CHIRSTMAS COLORING BOOK FOR KIDS

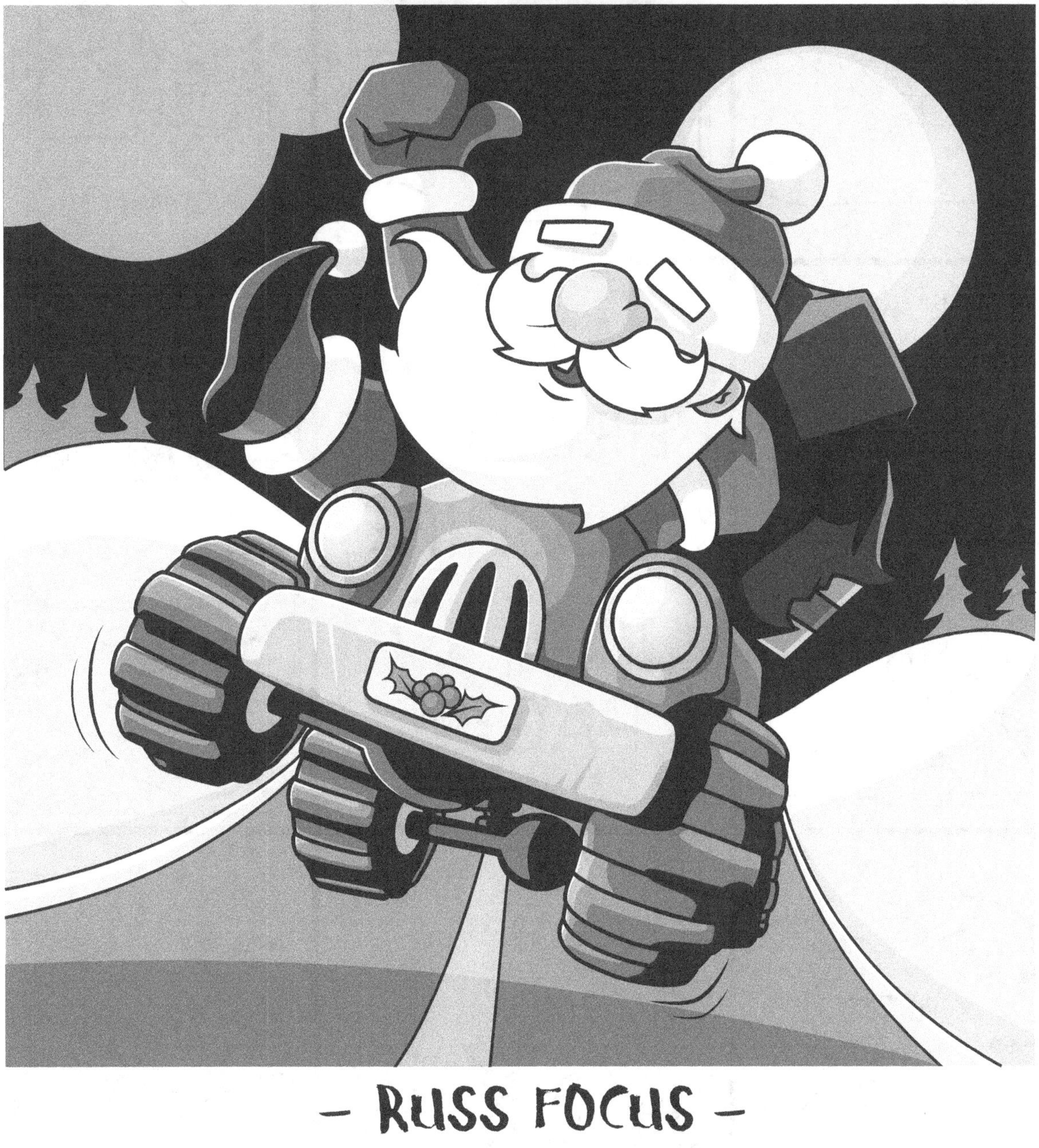

- RUSS FOCUS -

ISBN: 9781706632887

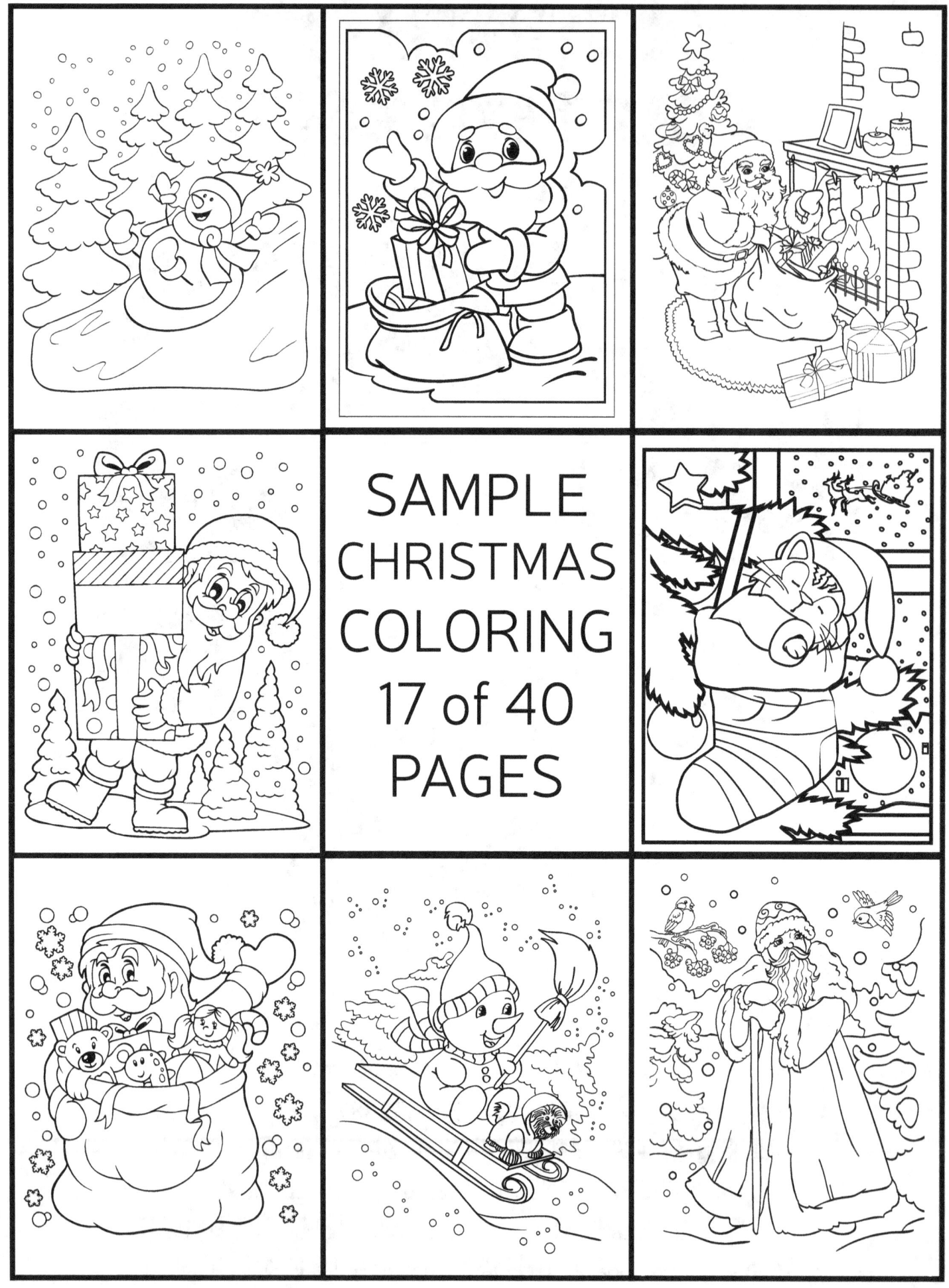

SAMPLE
CHRISTMAS
COLORING
17 of 40
PAGES

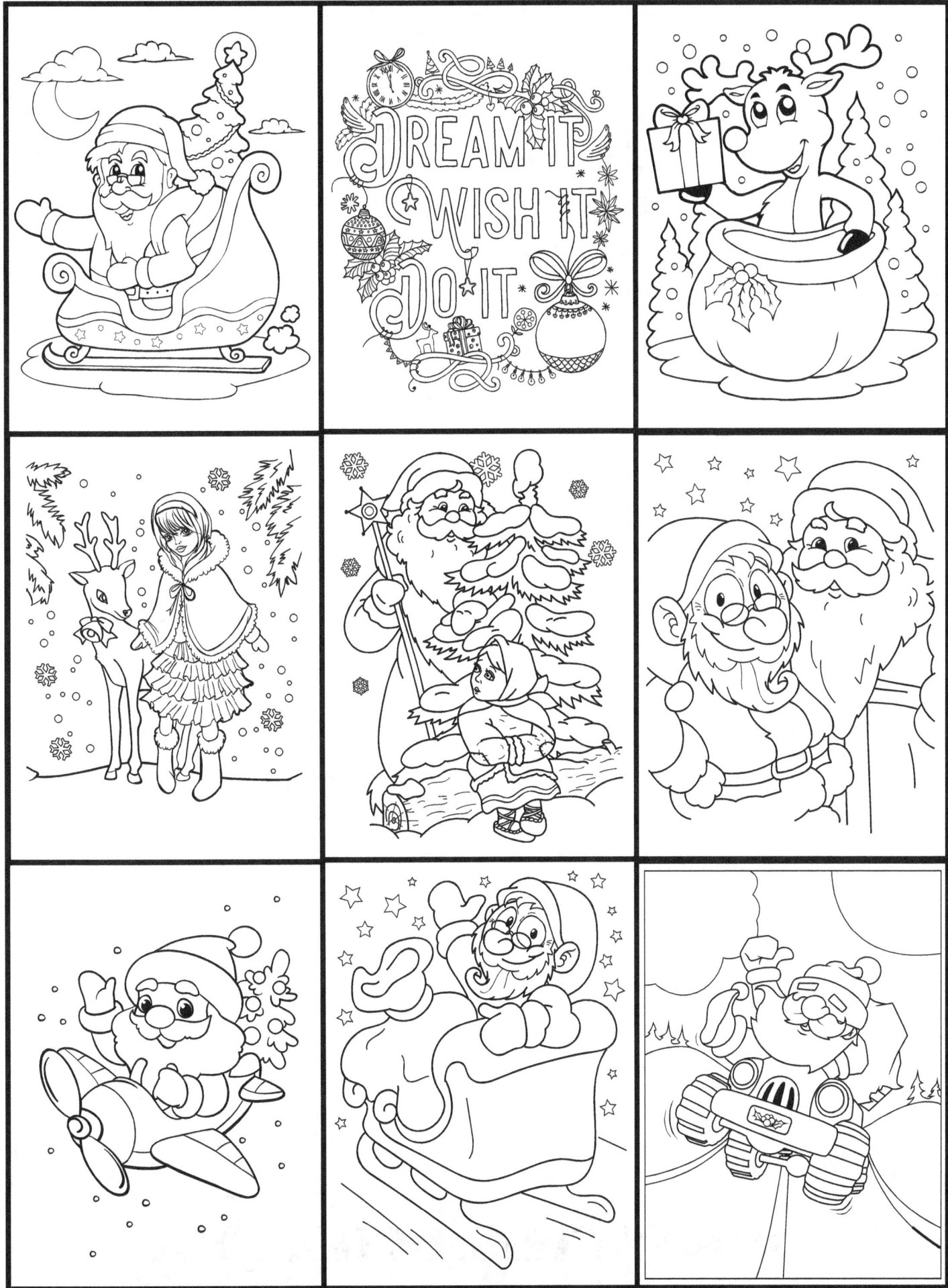

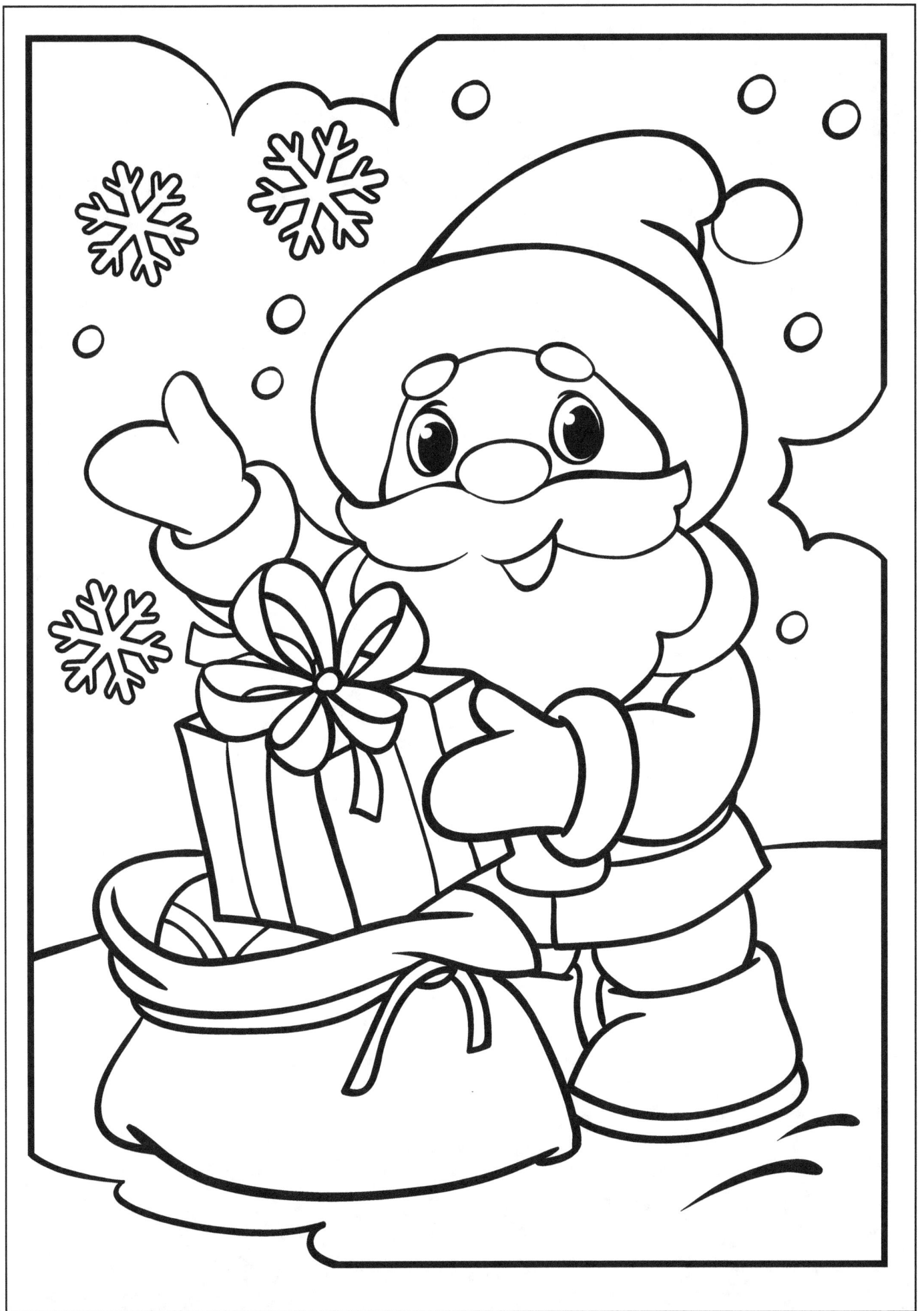

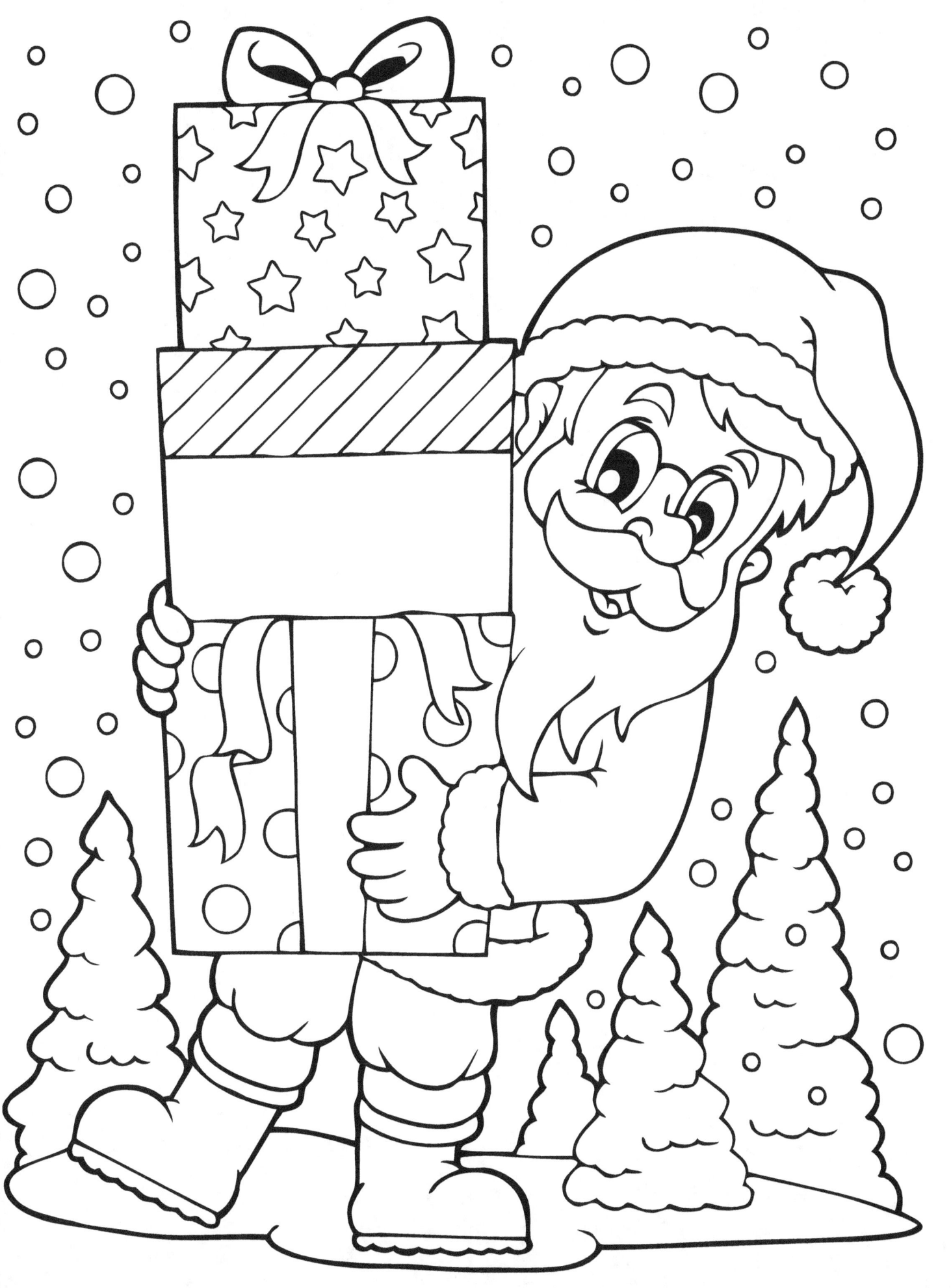

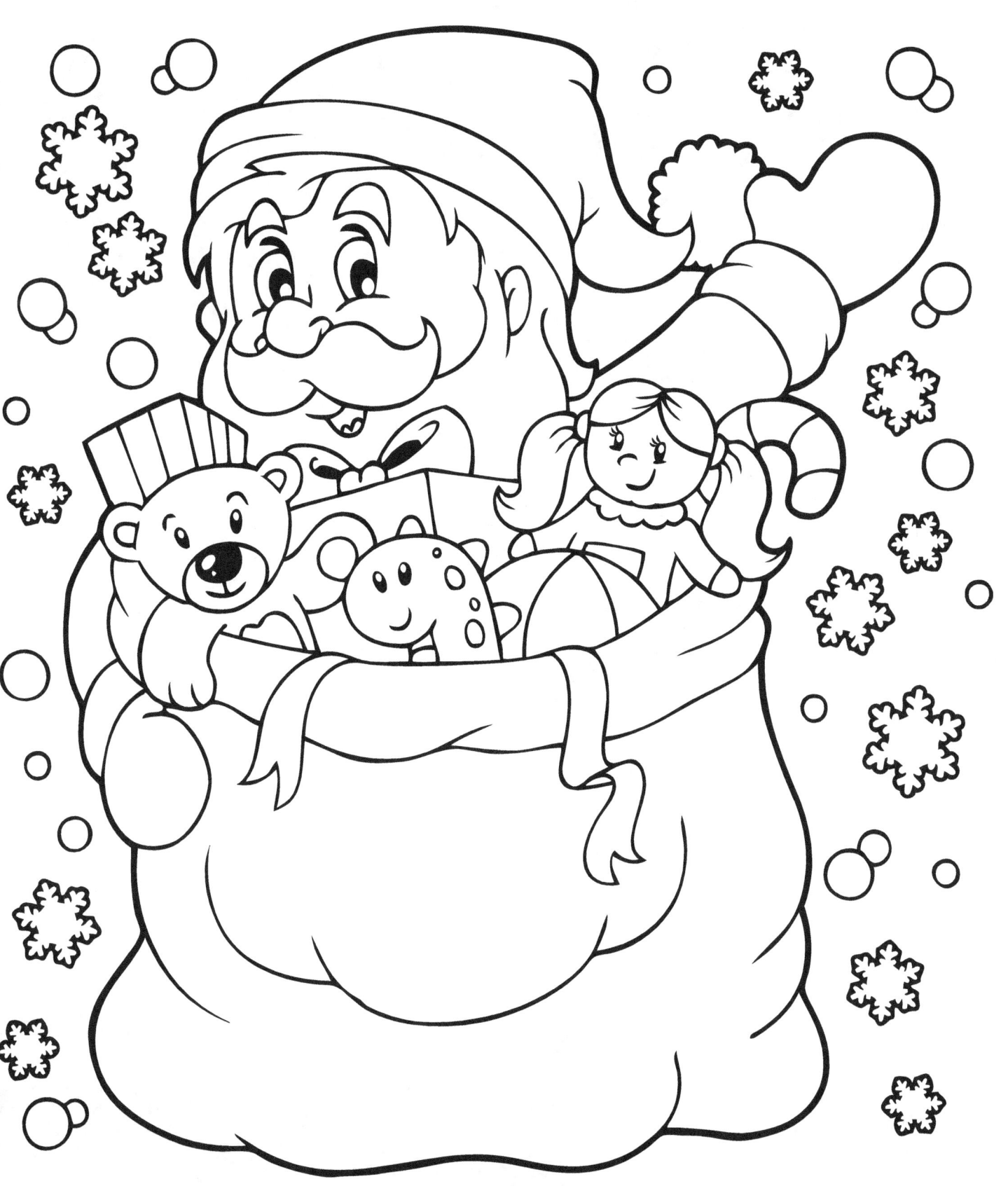

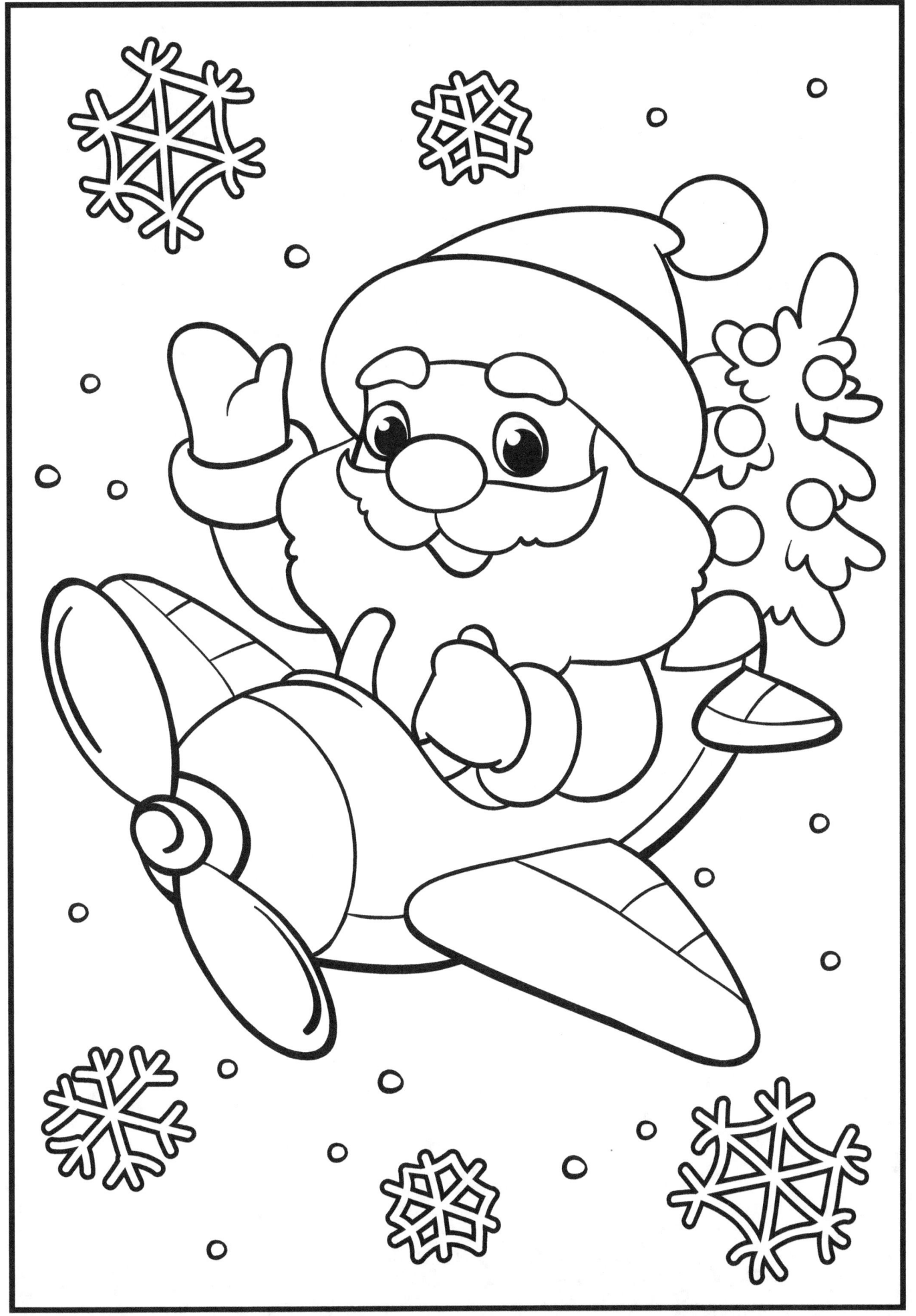

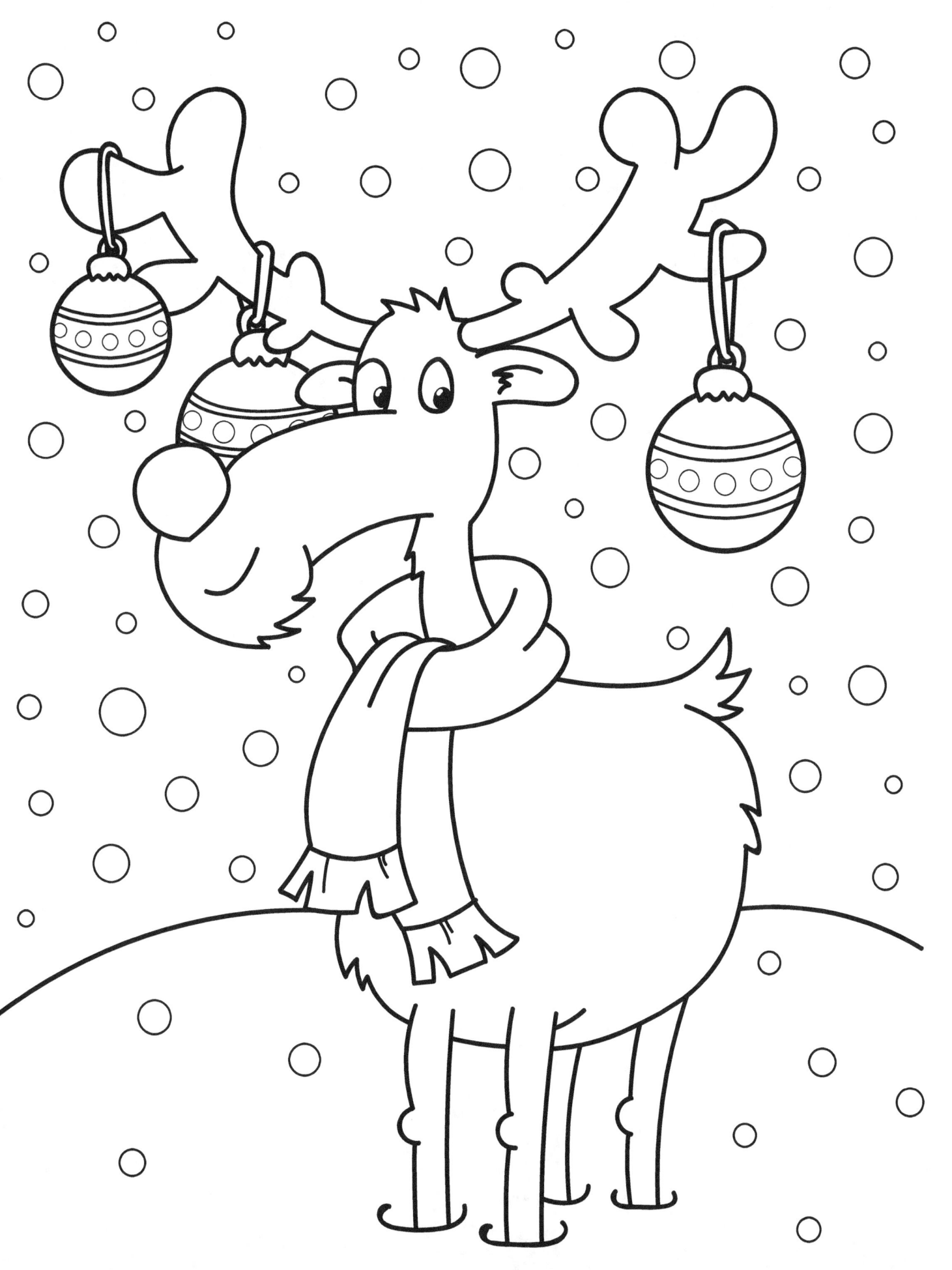

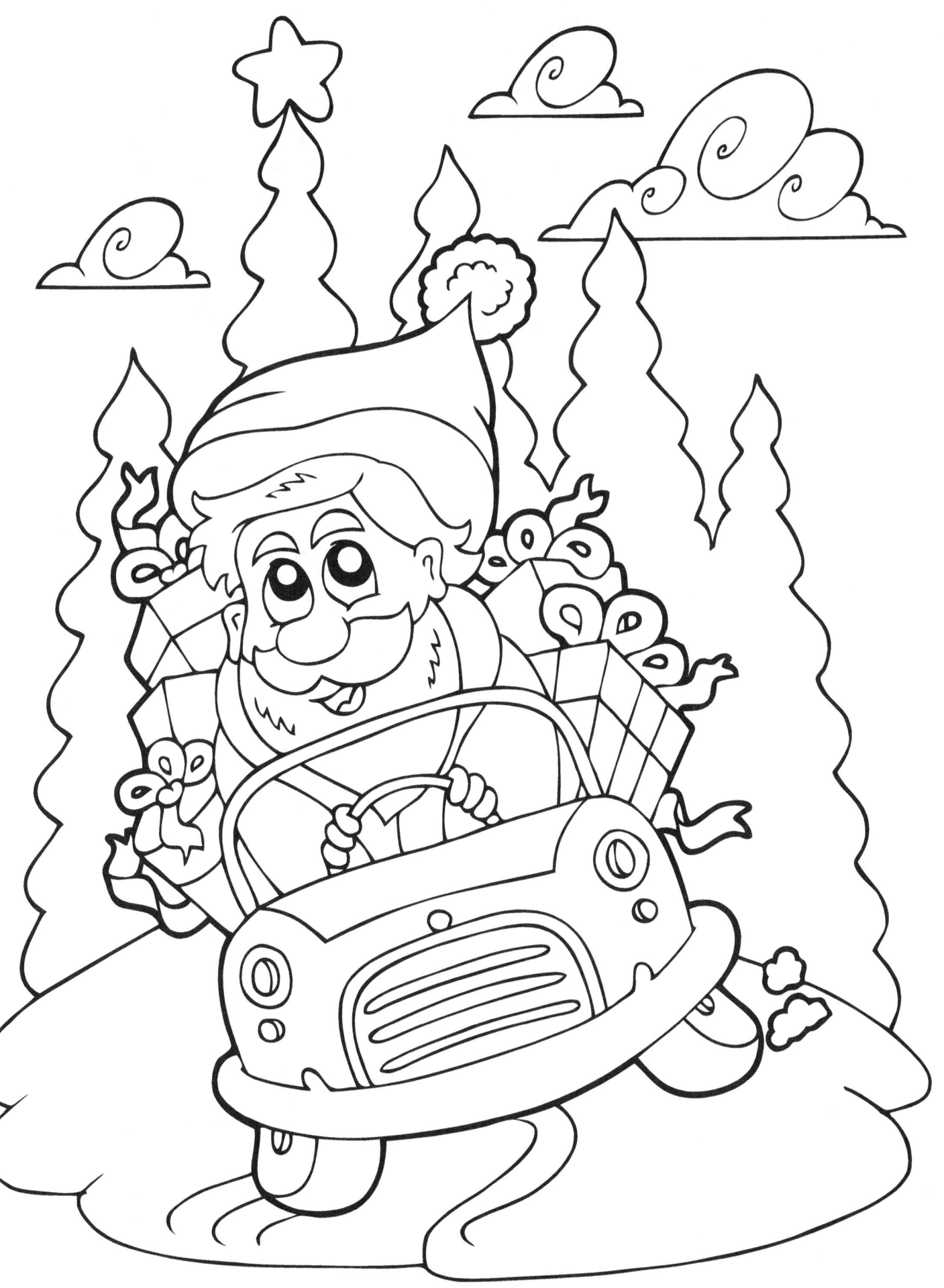

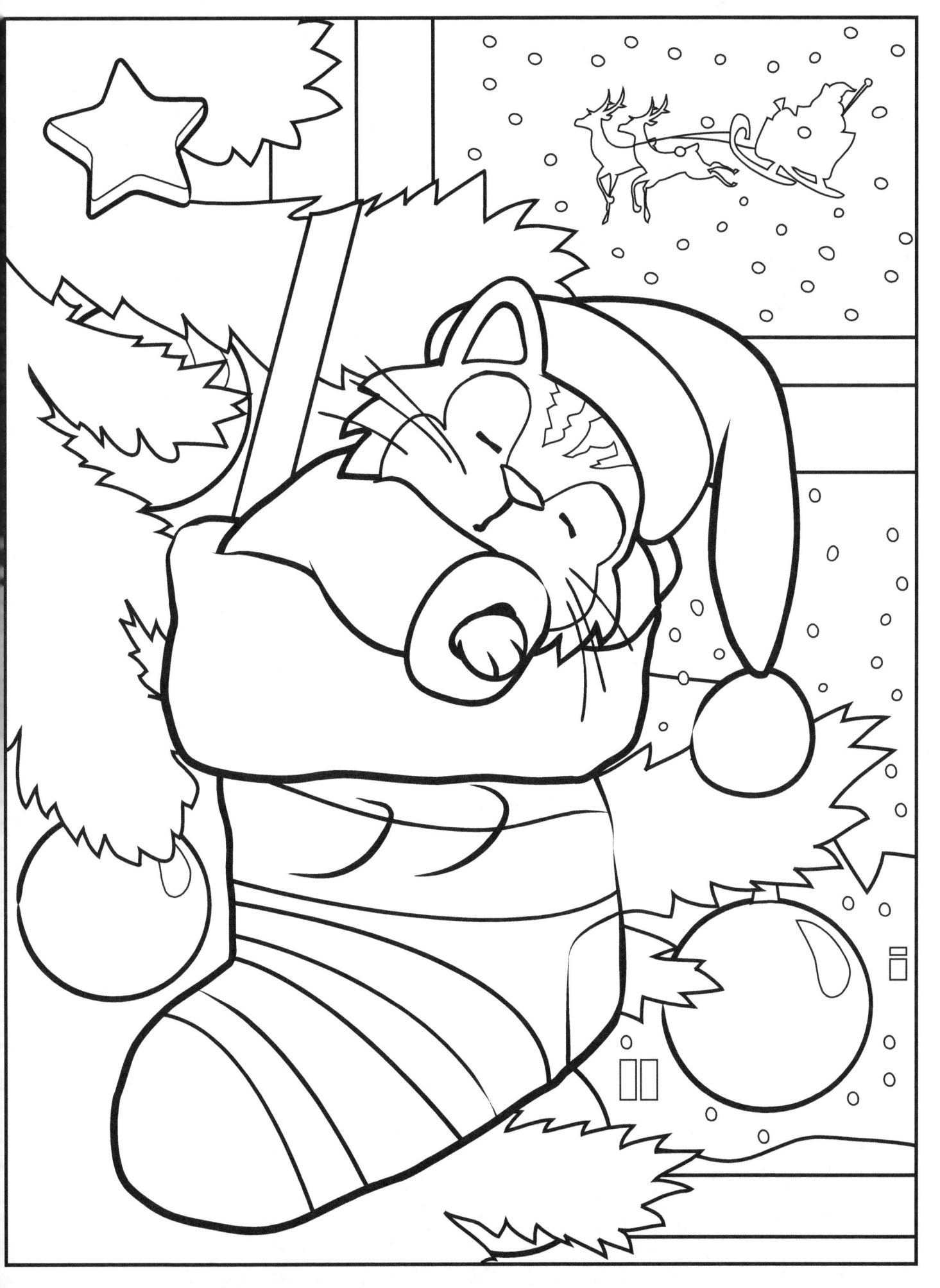

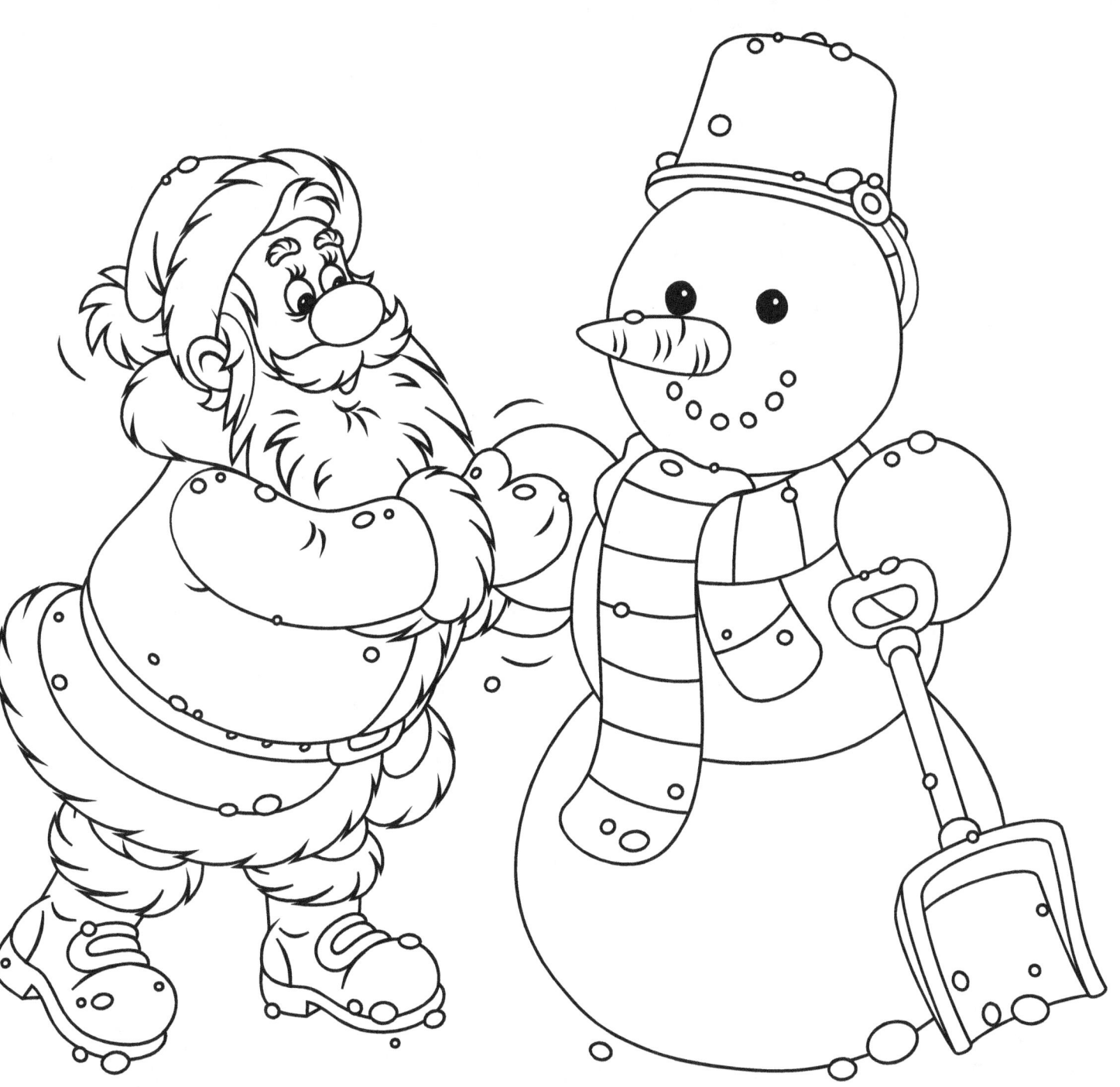

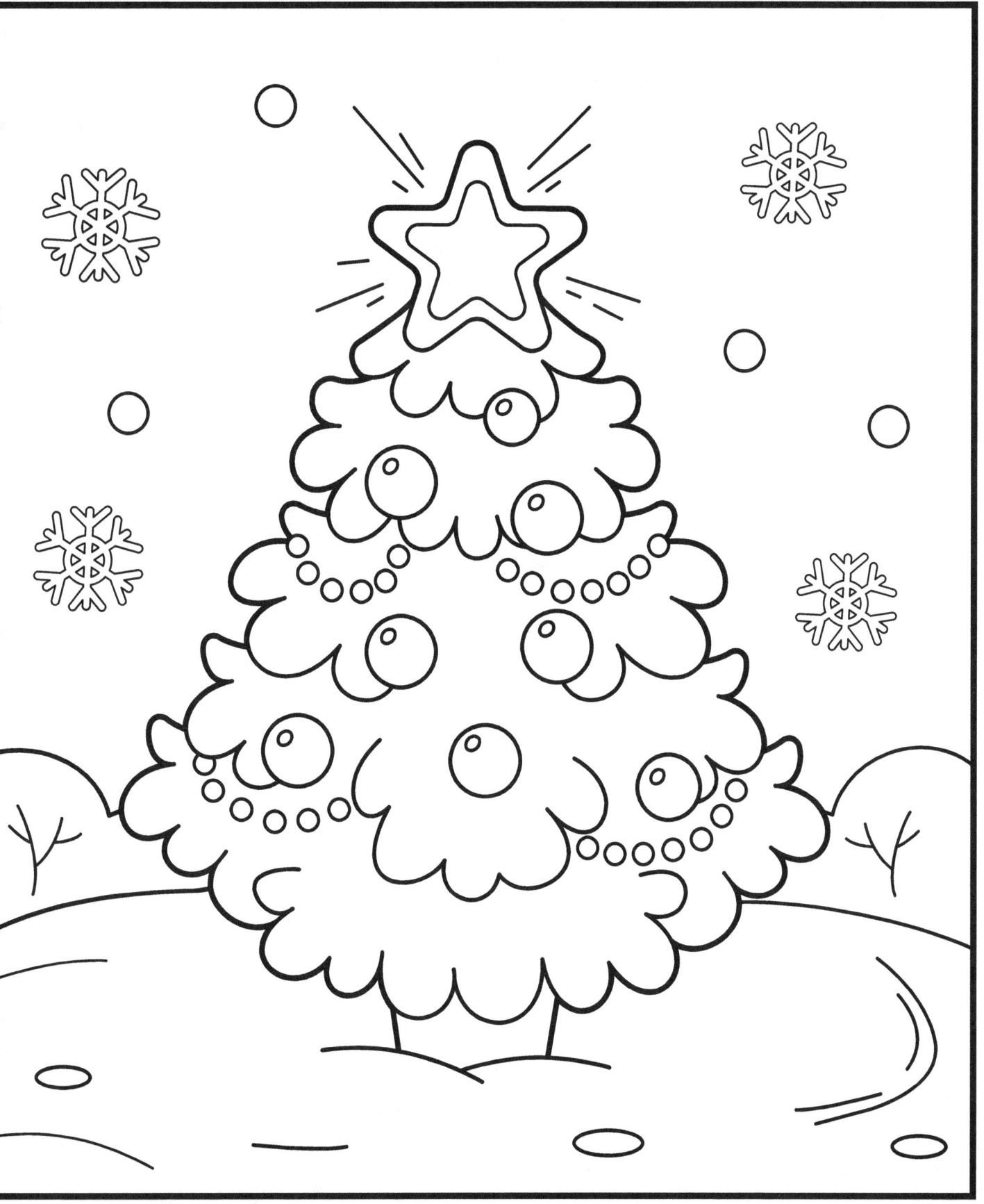

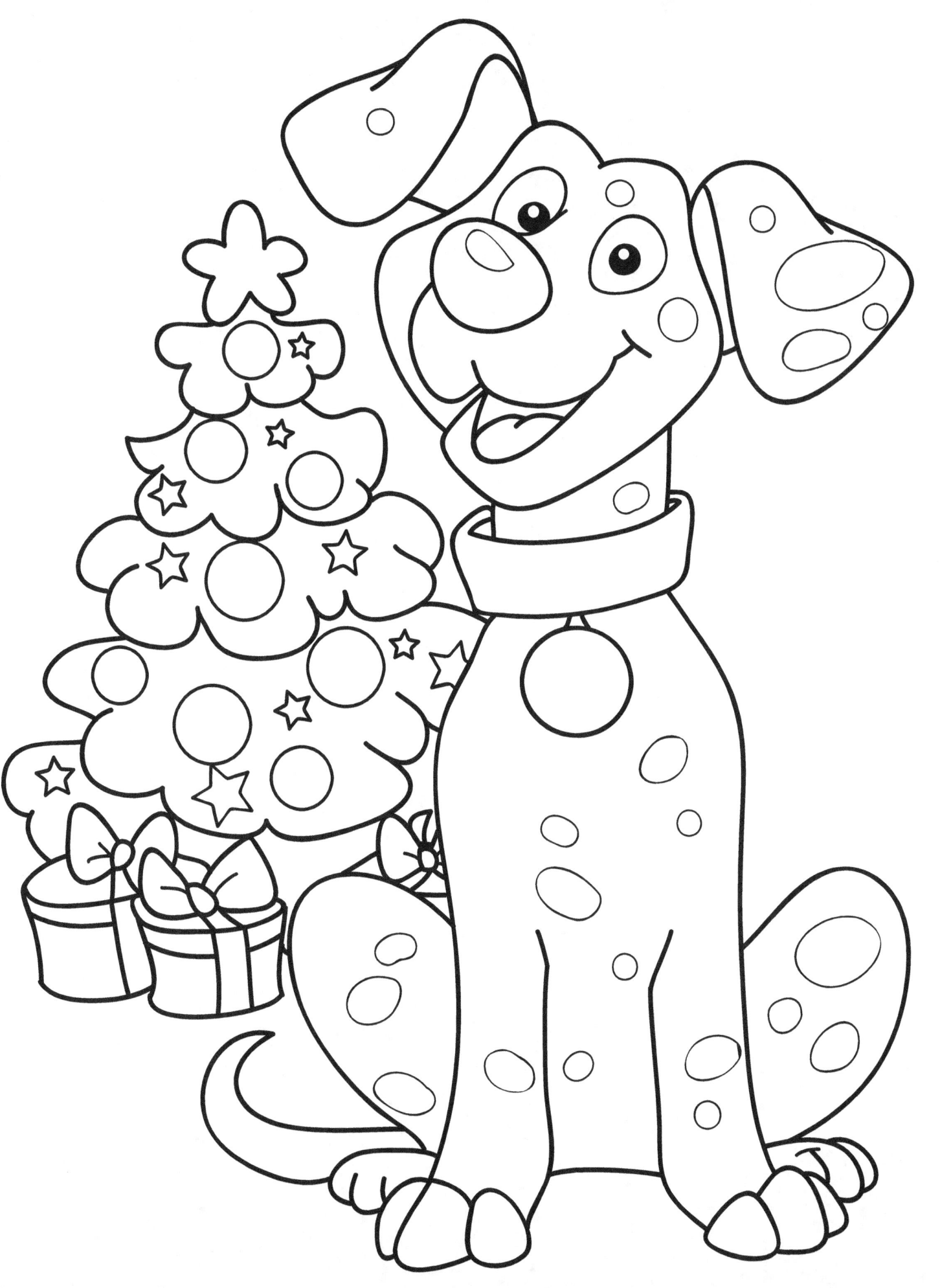

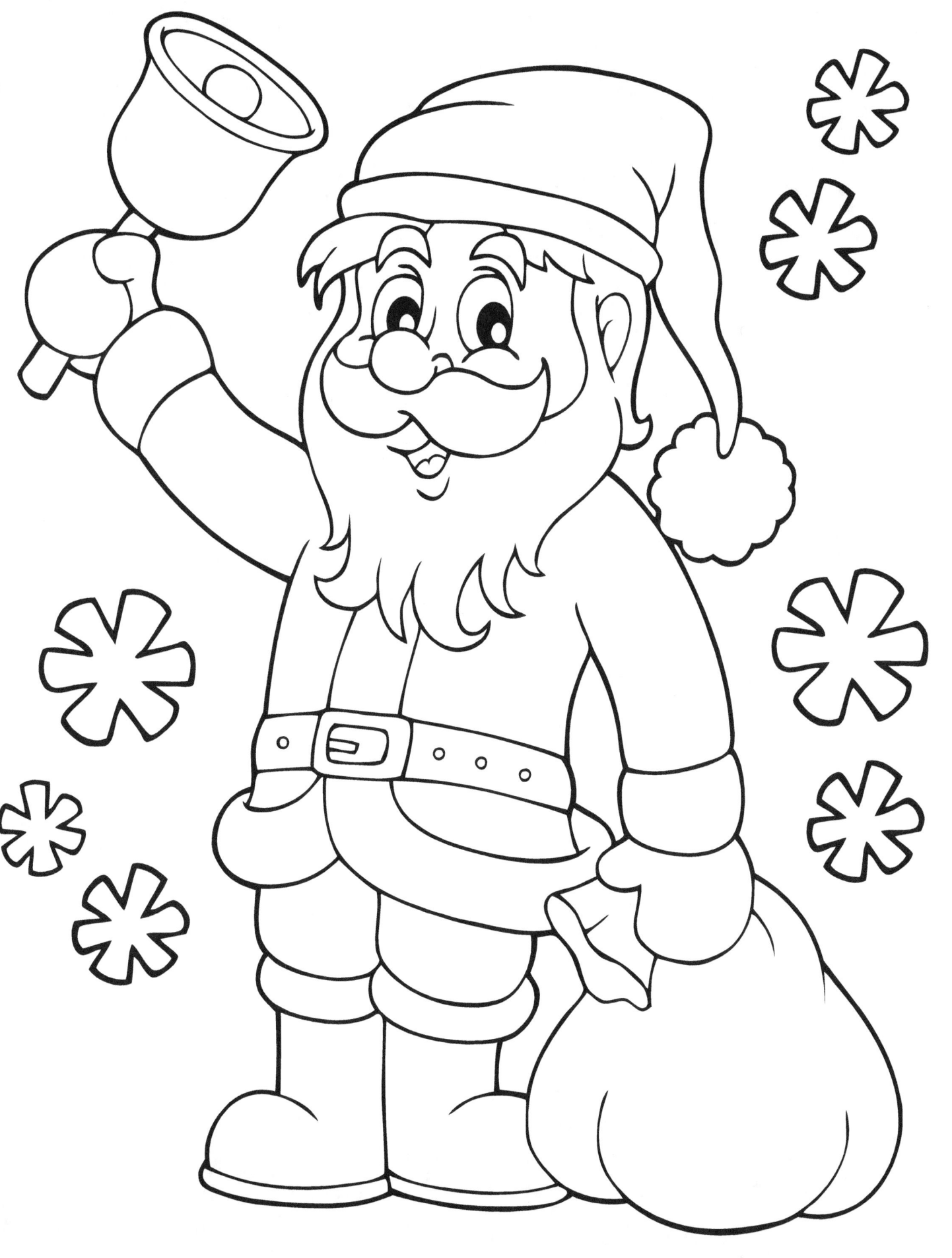

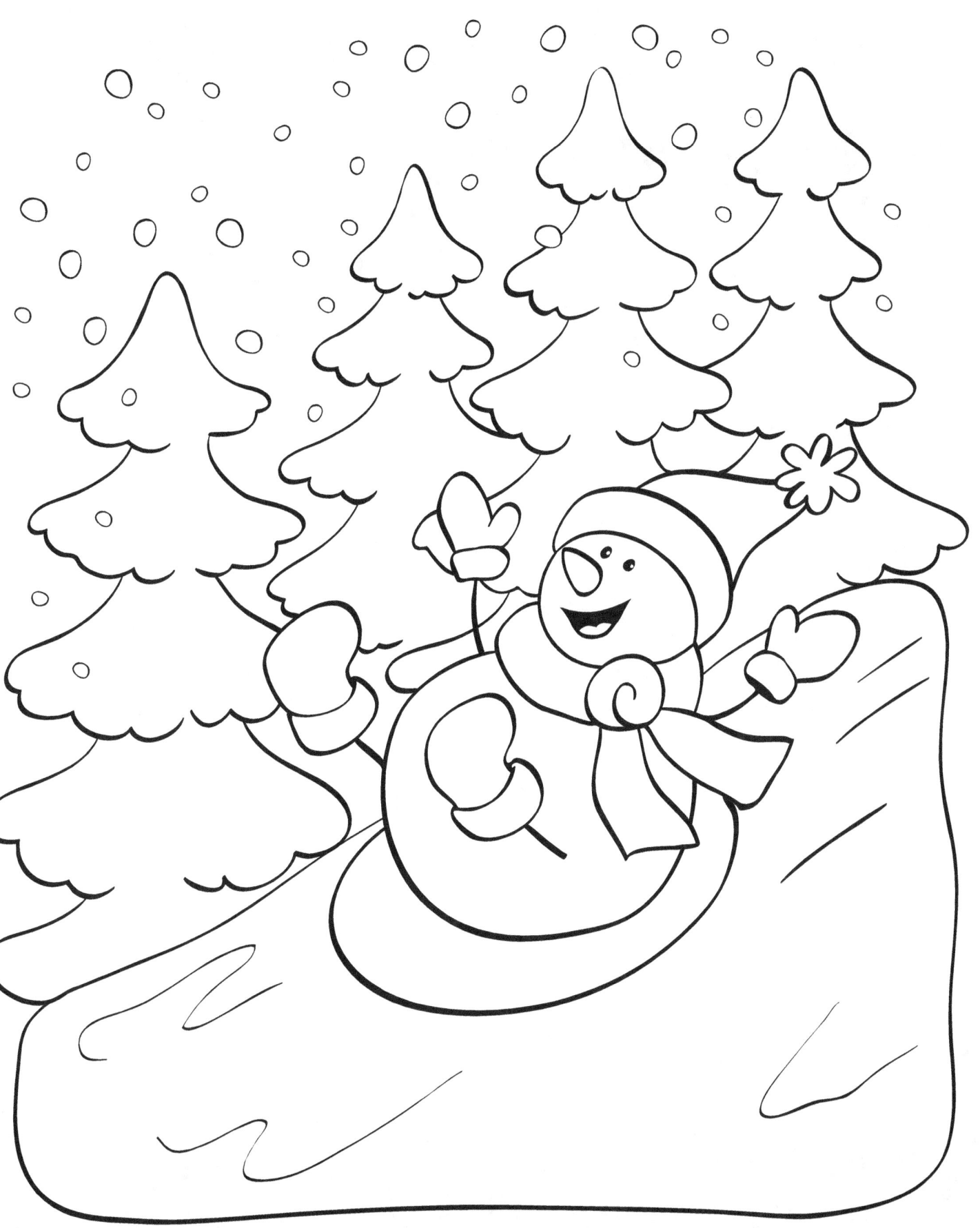

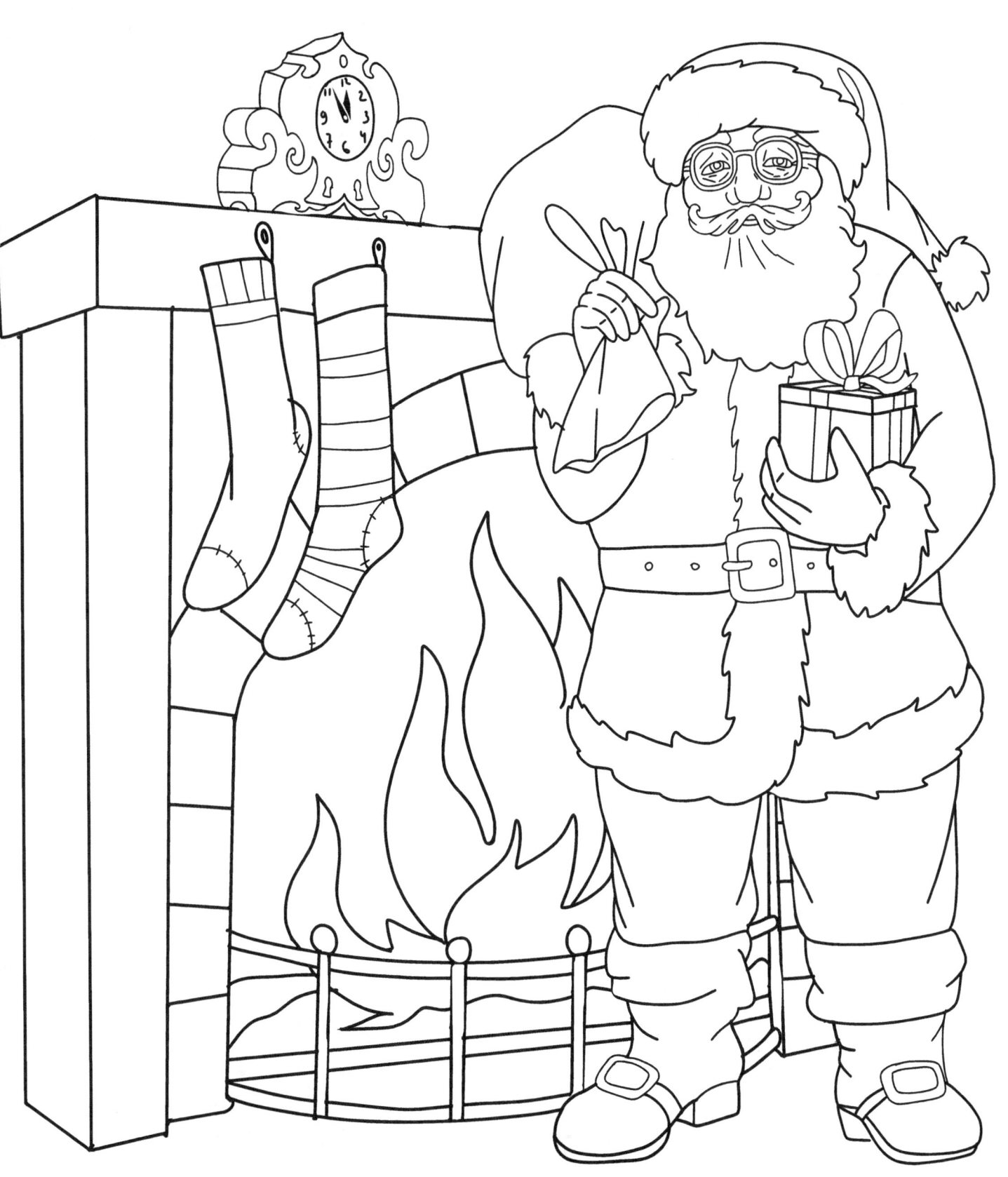

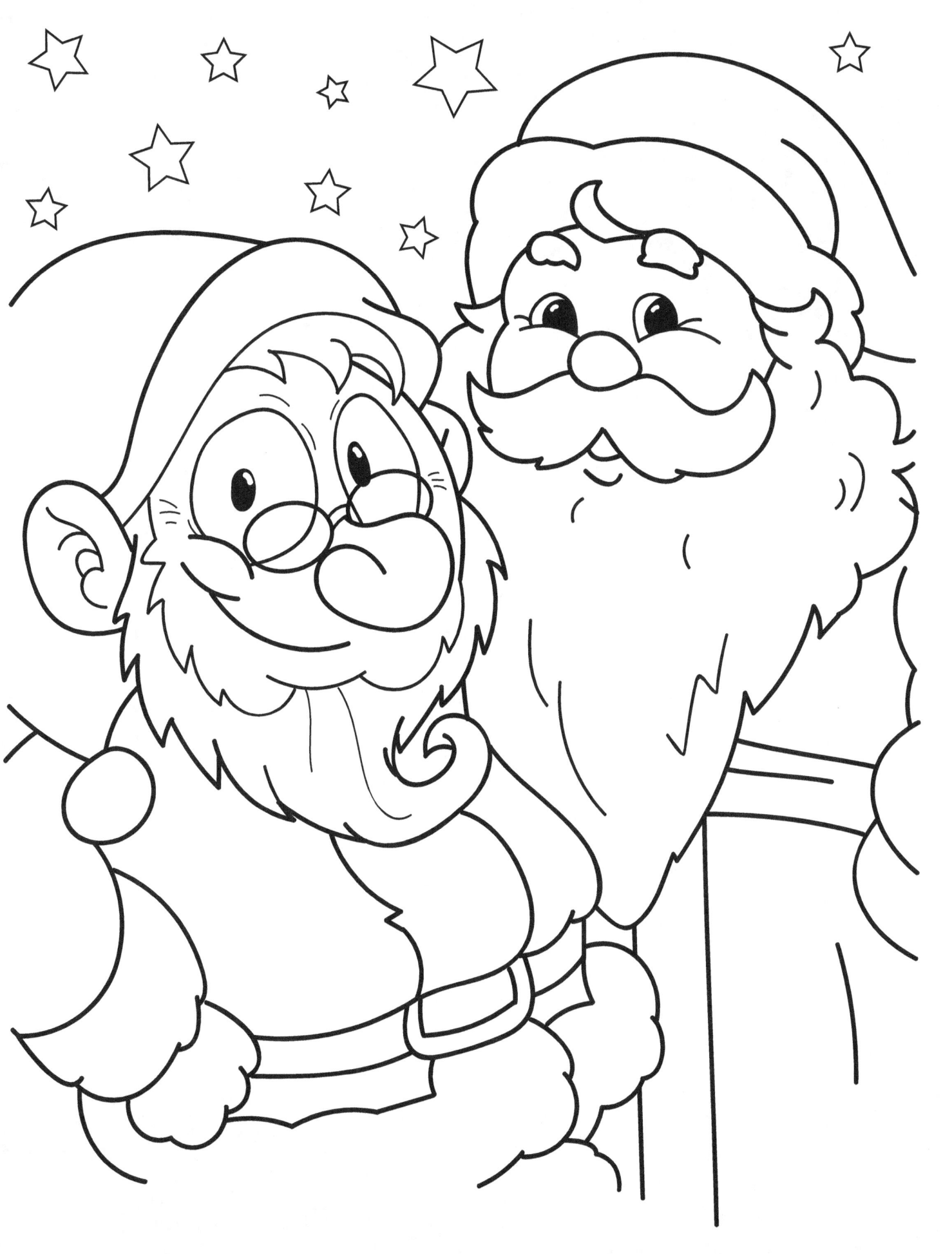

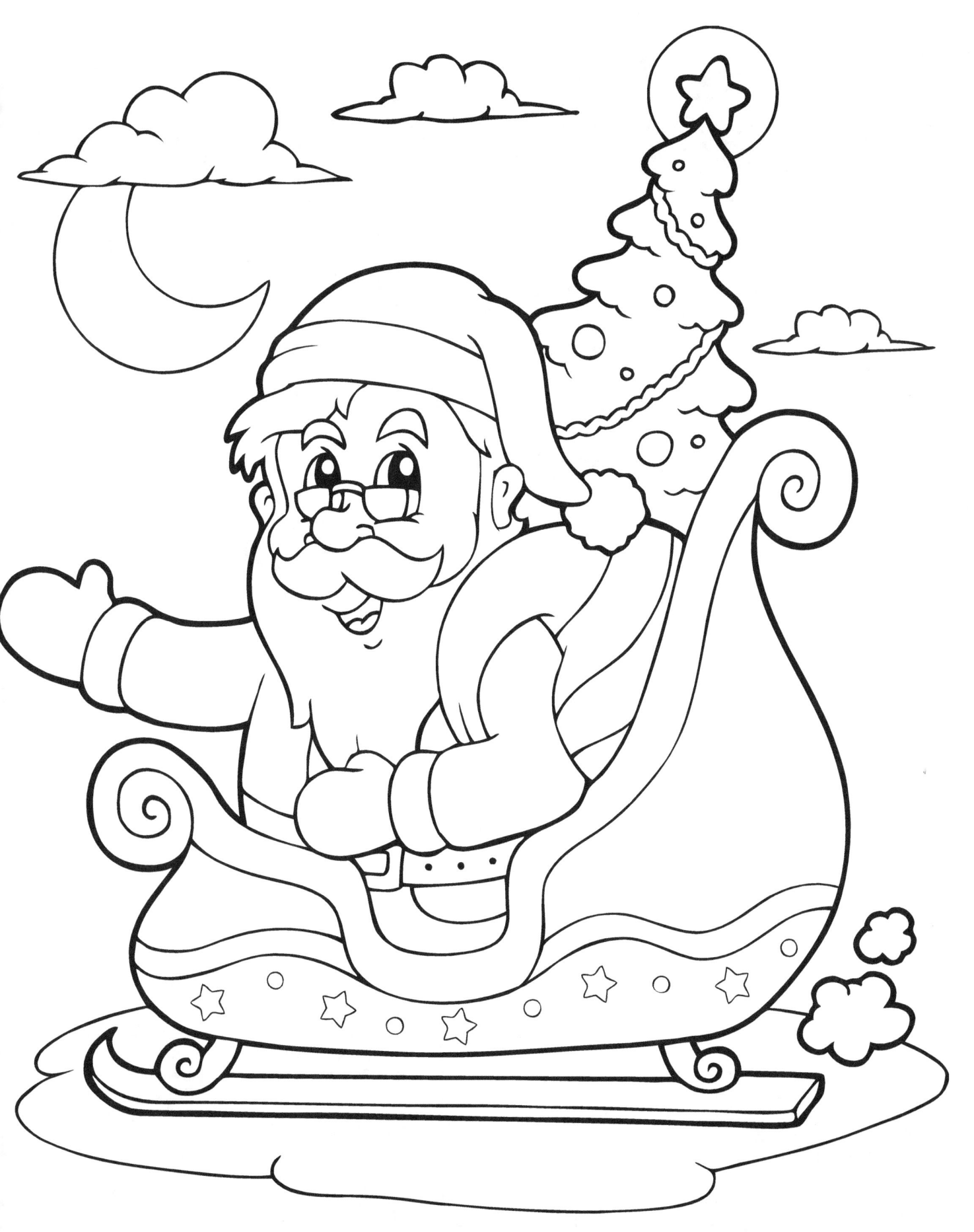

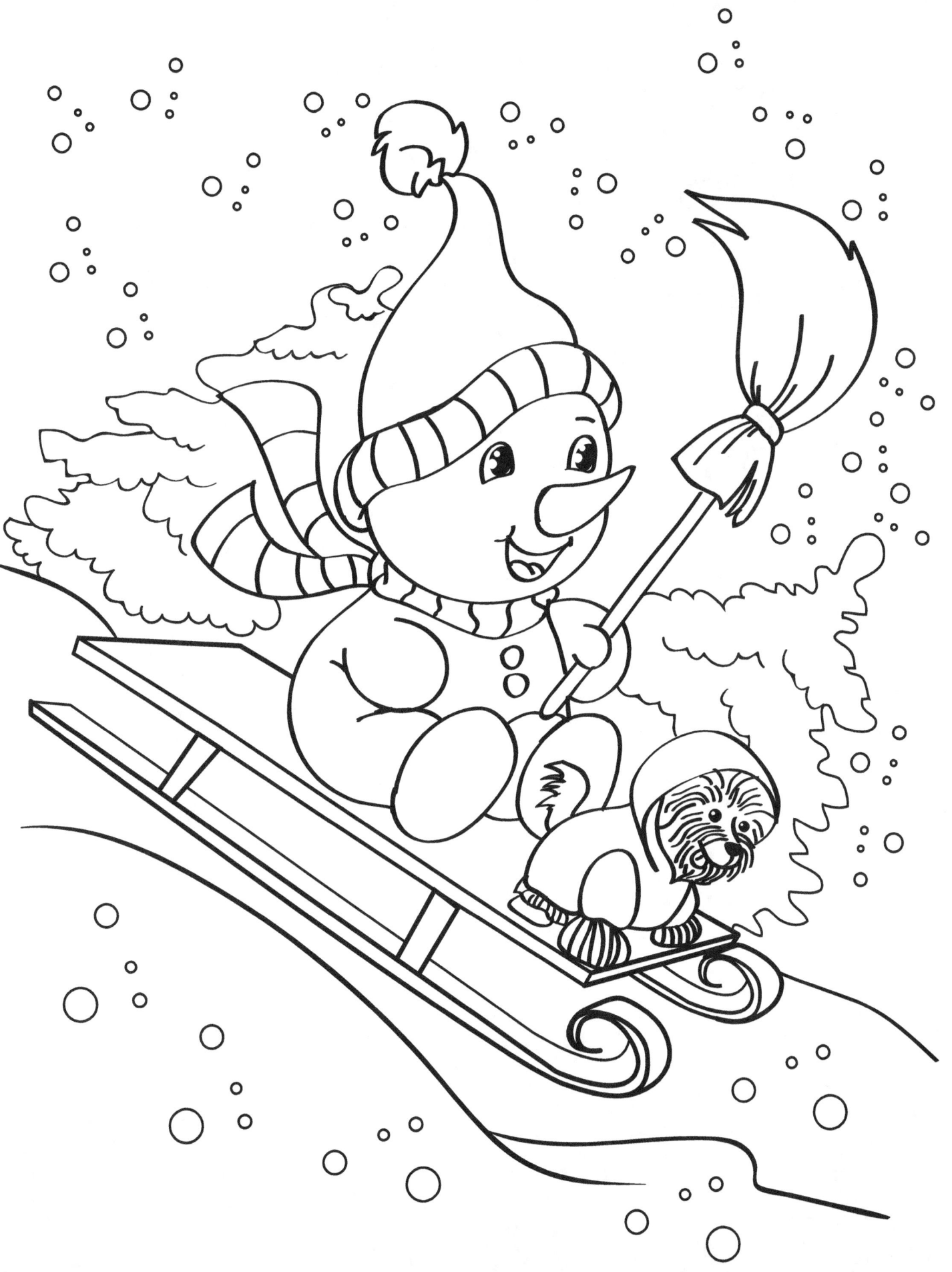

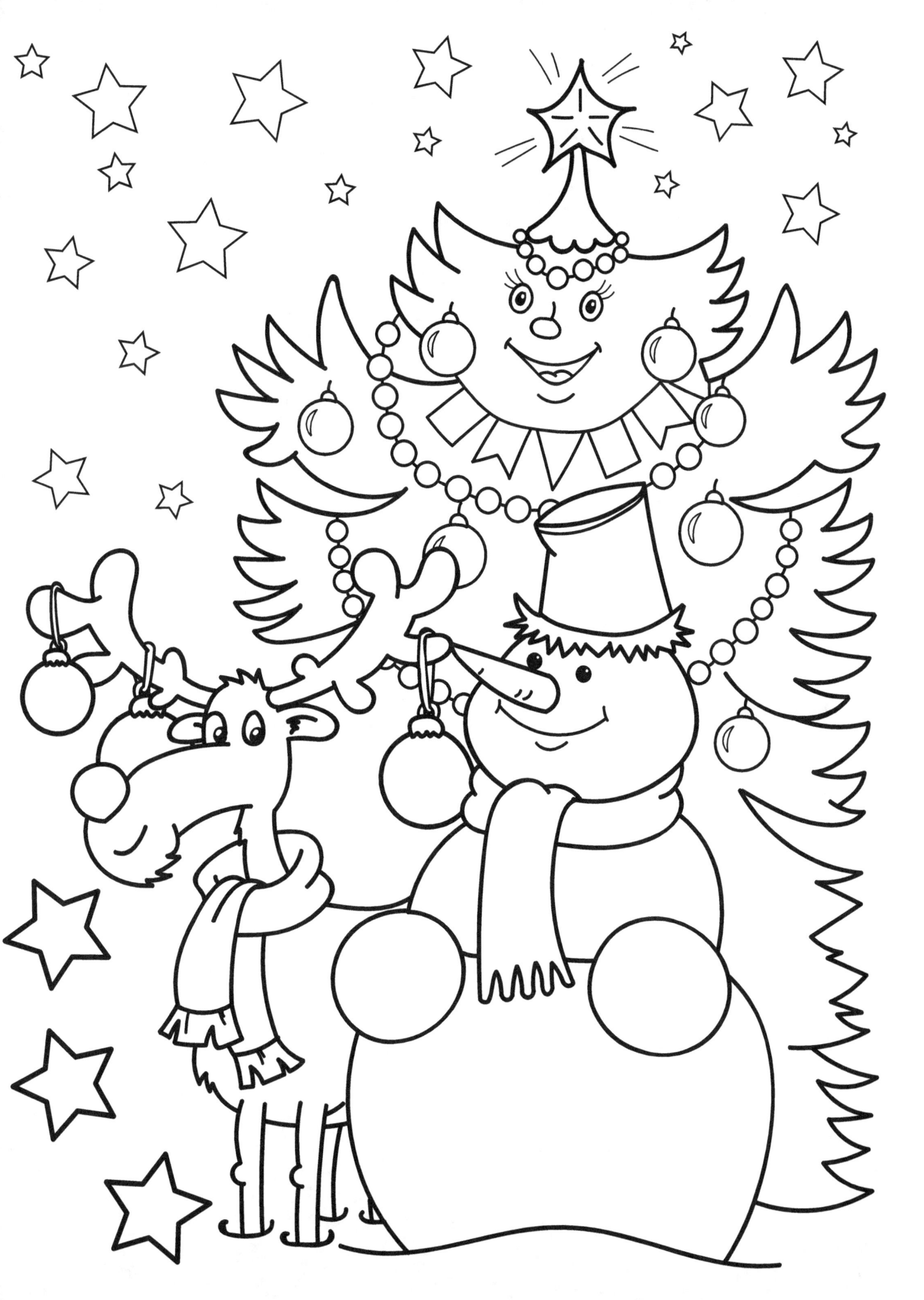

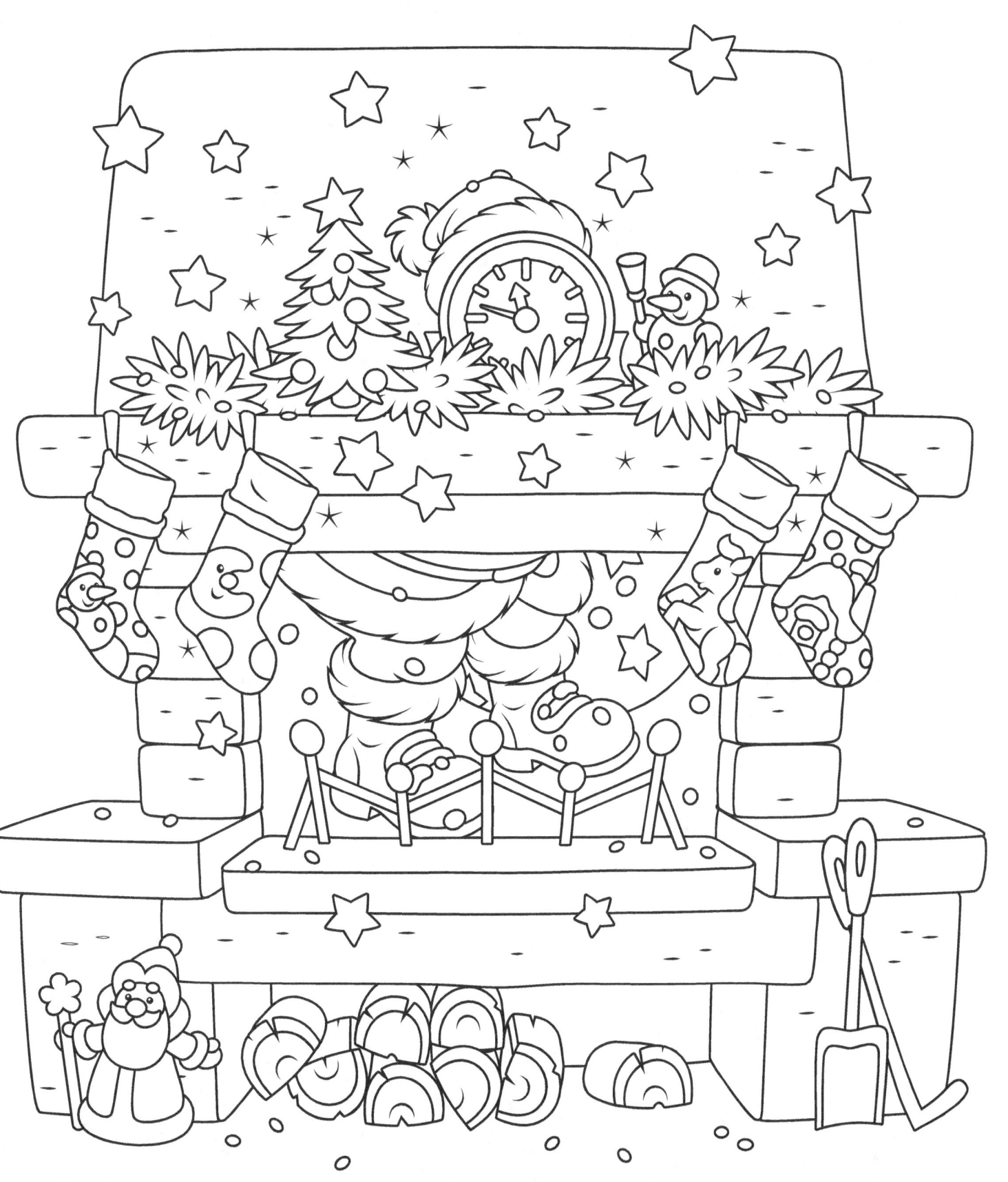

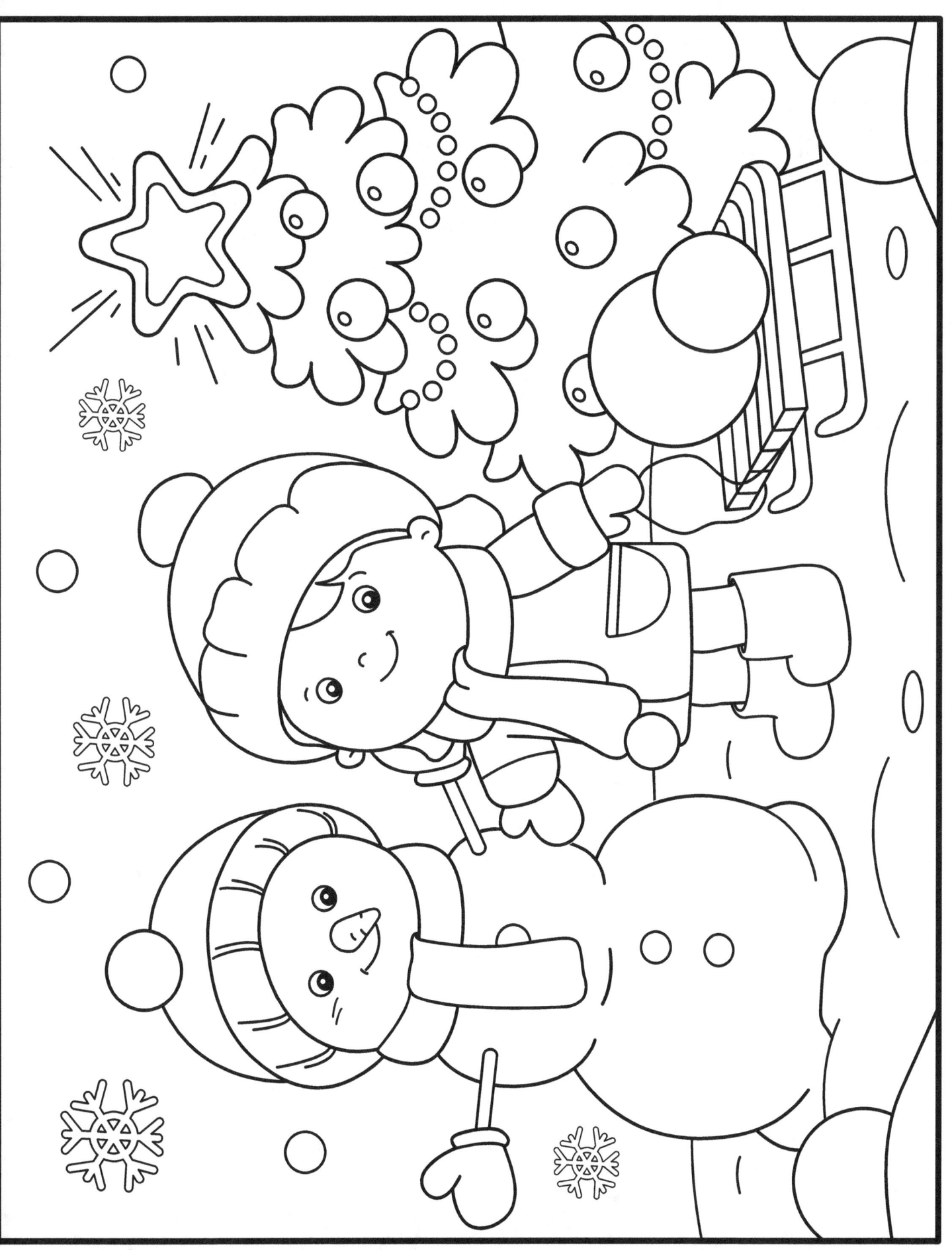

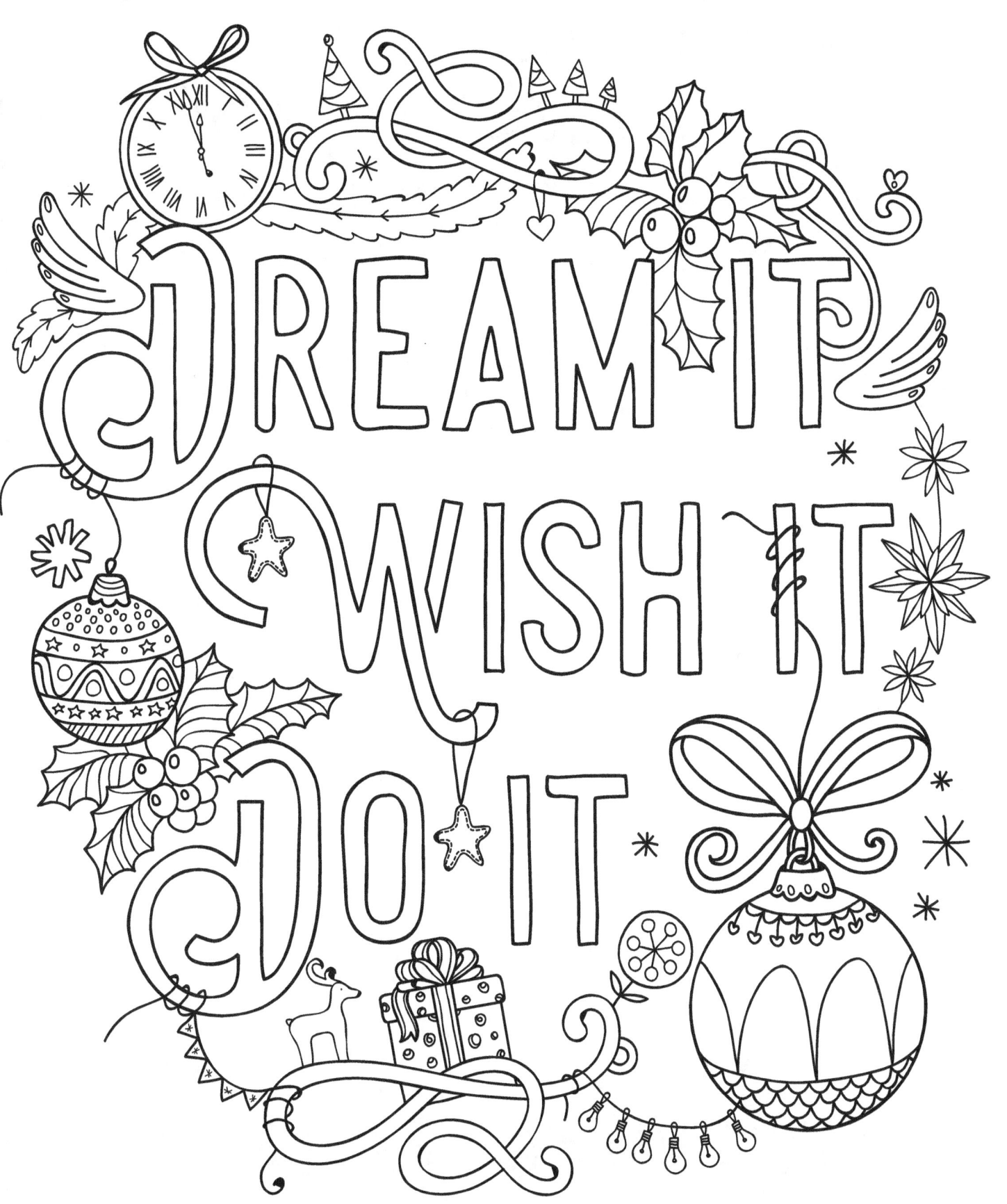

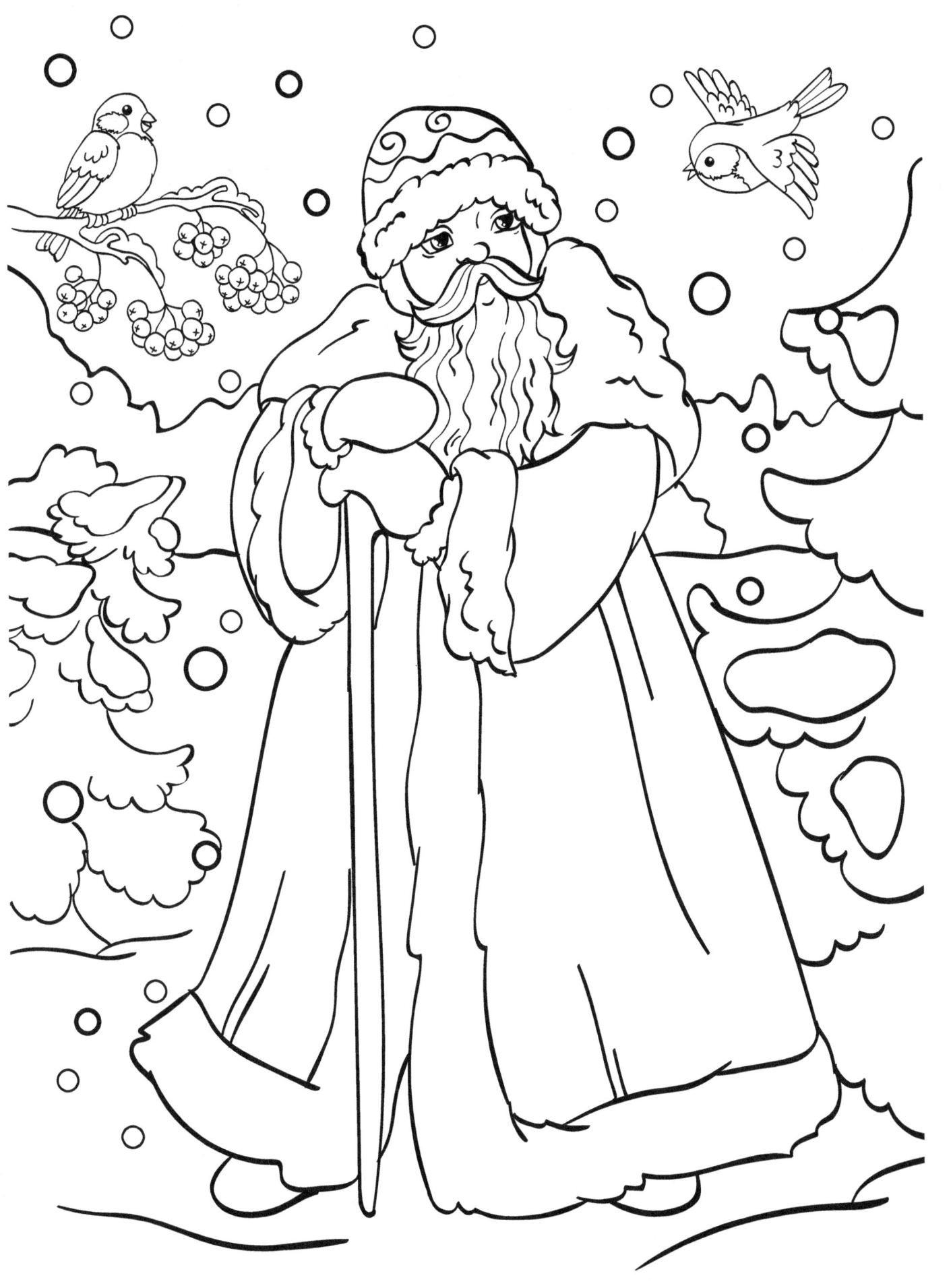

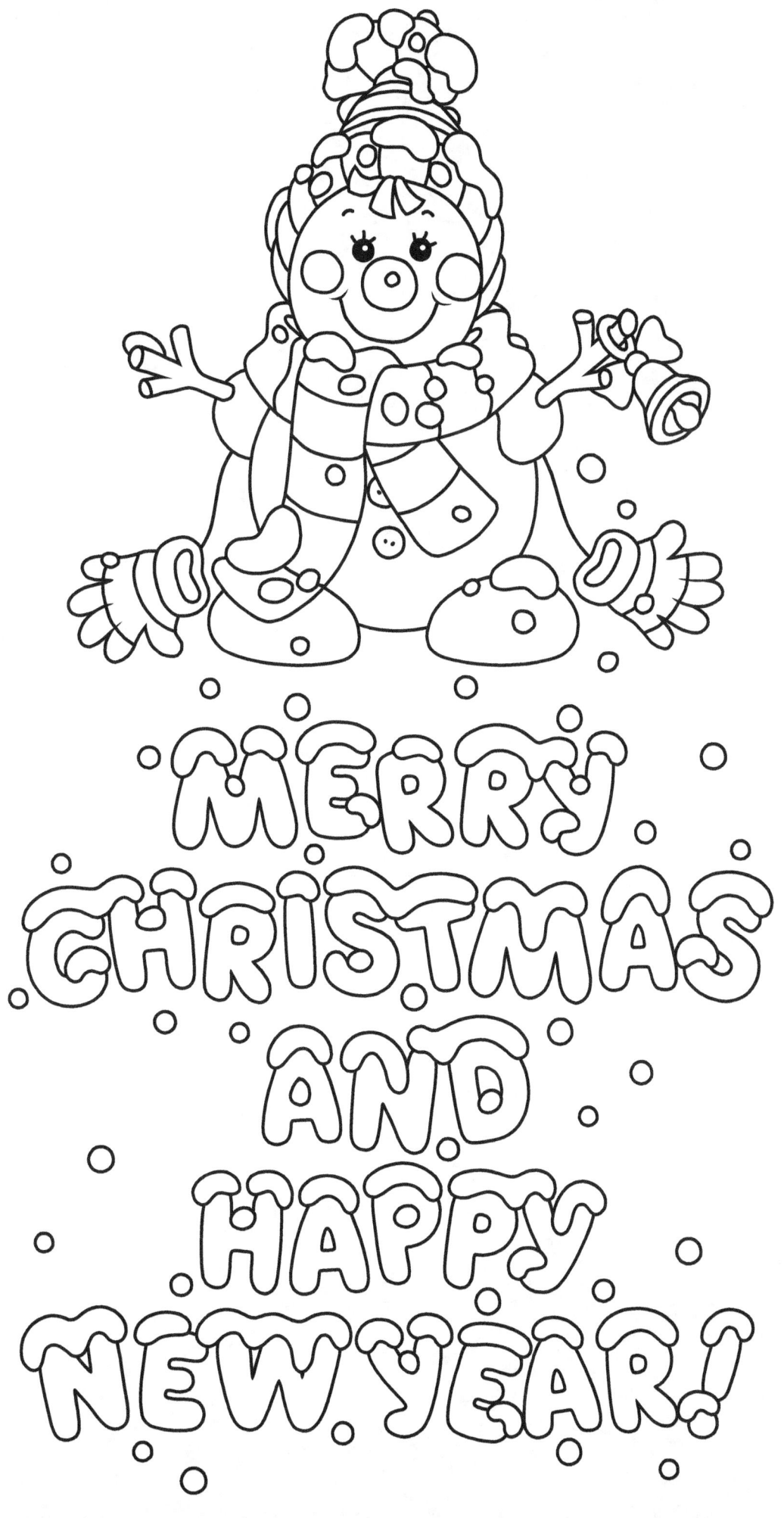

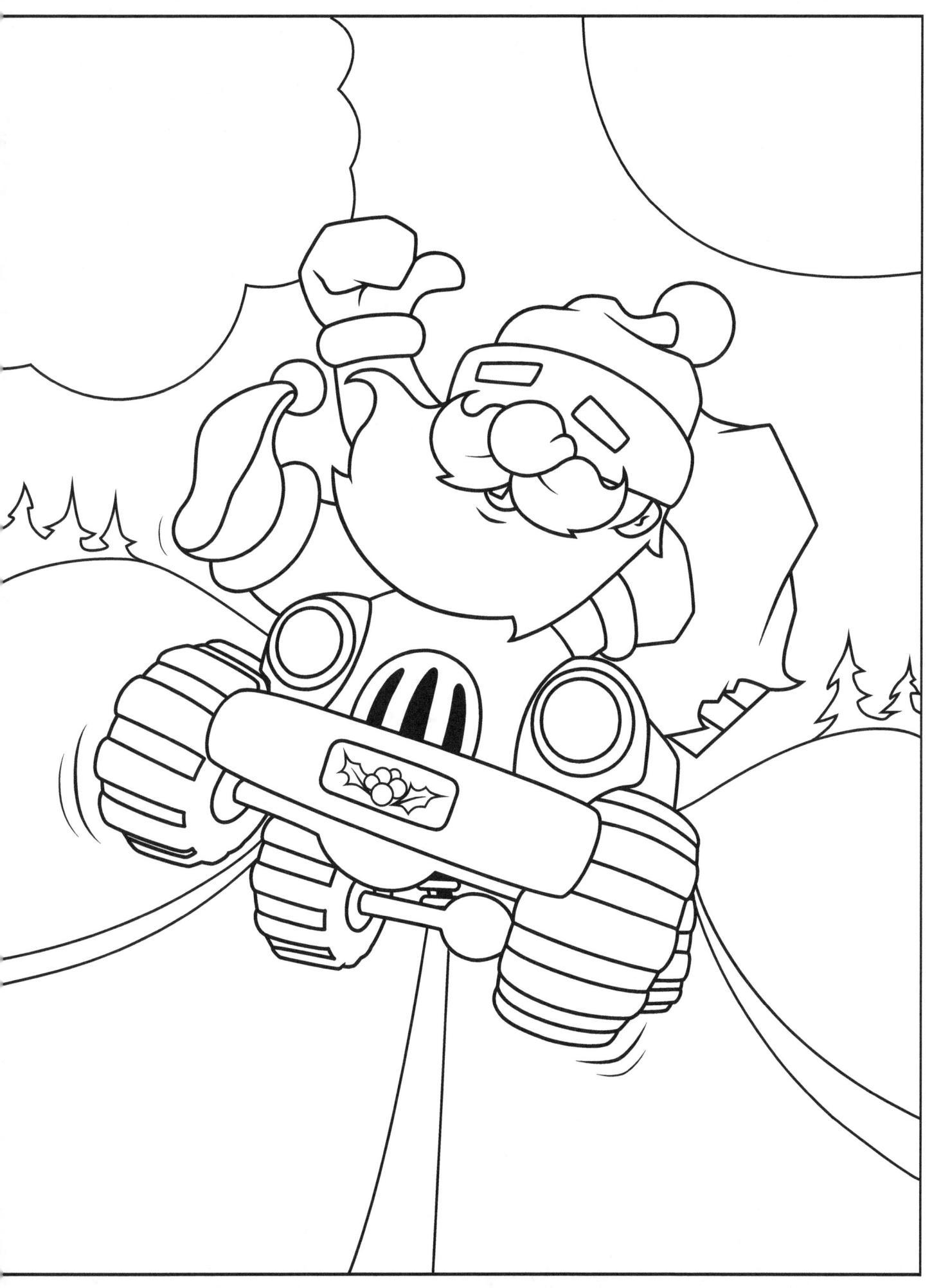

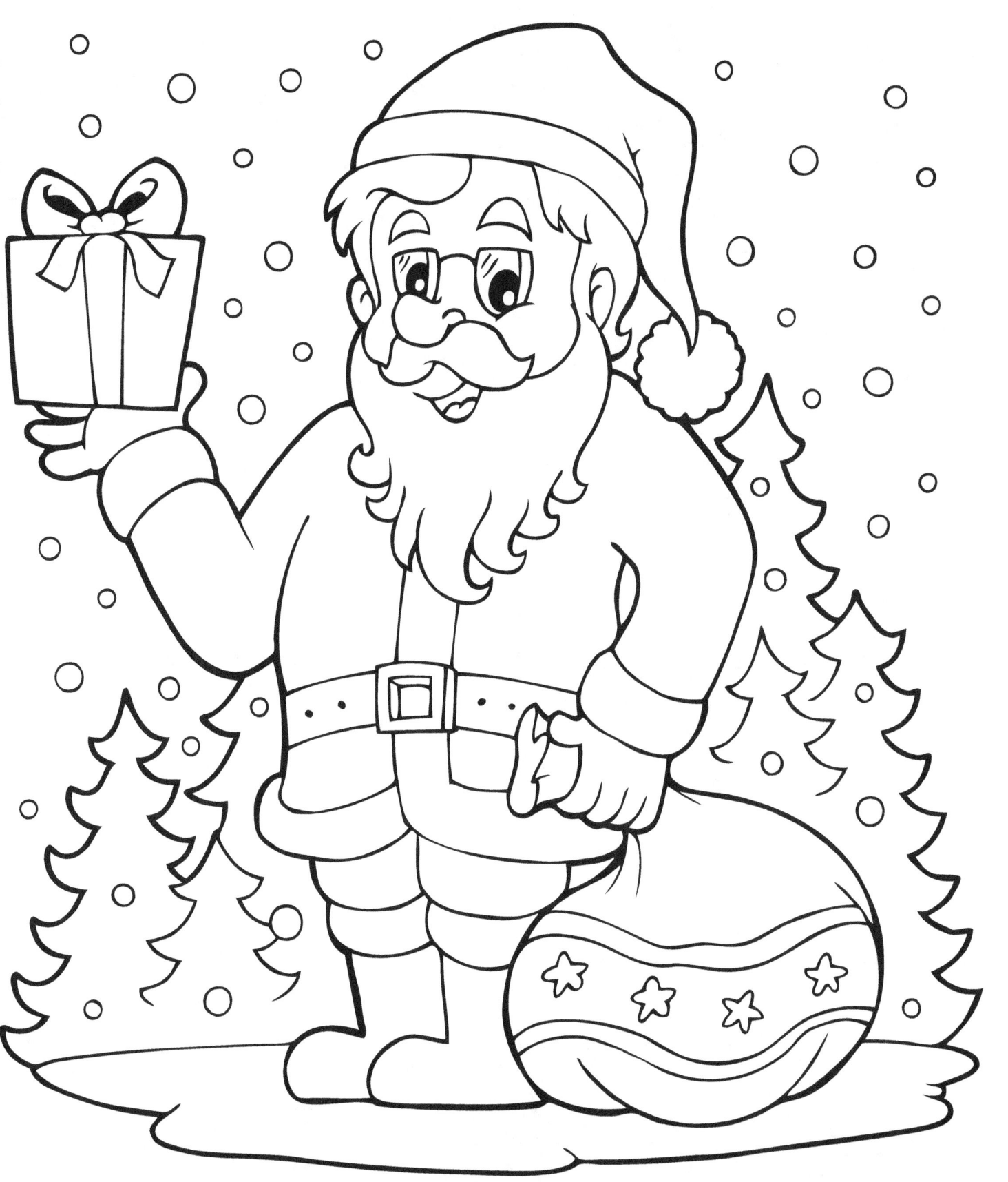

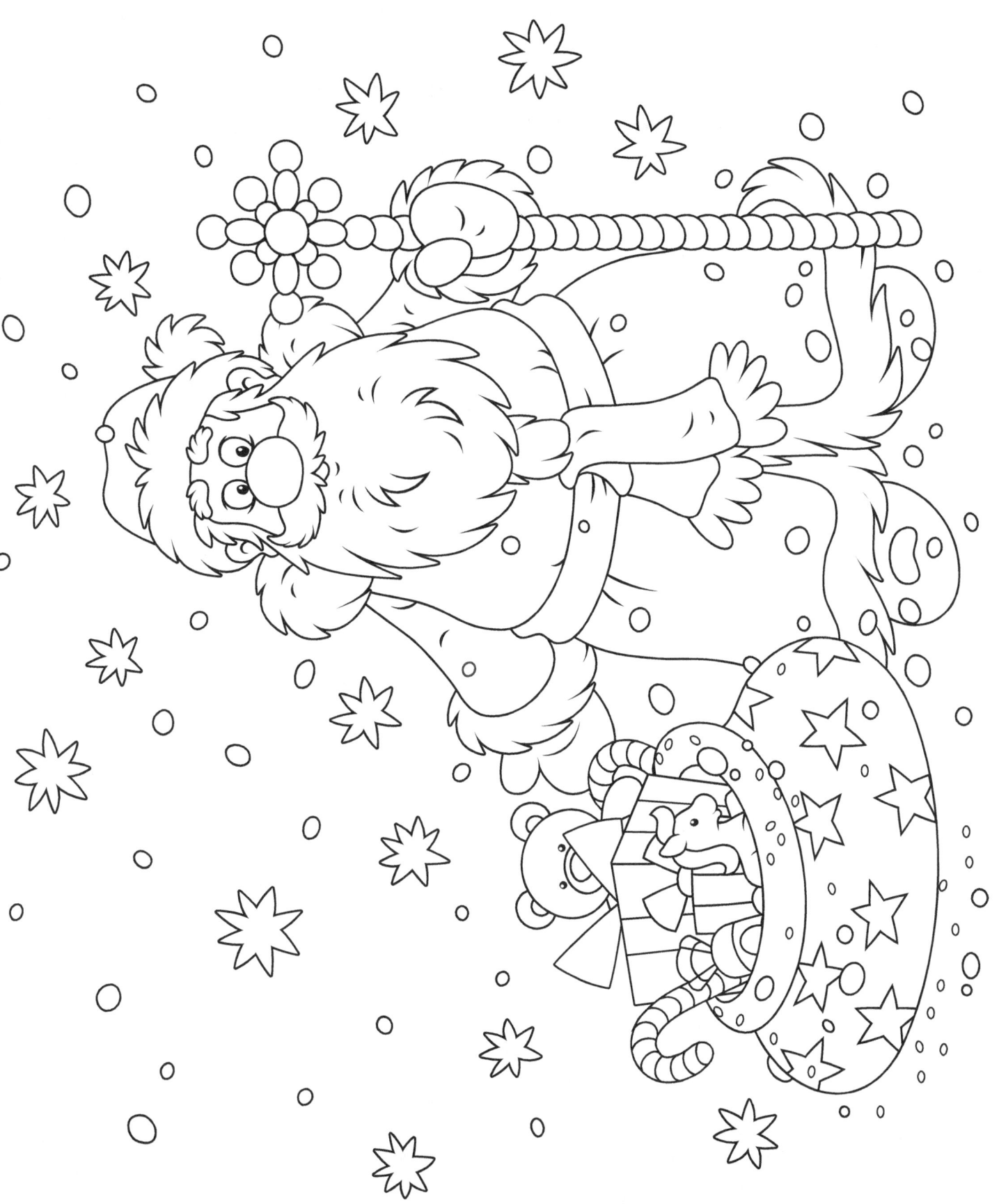

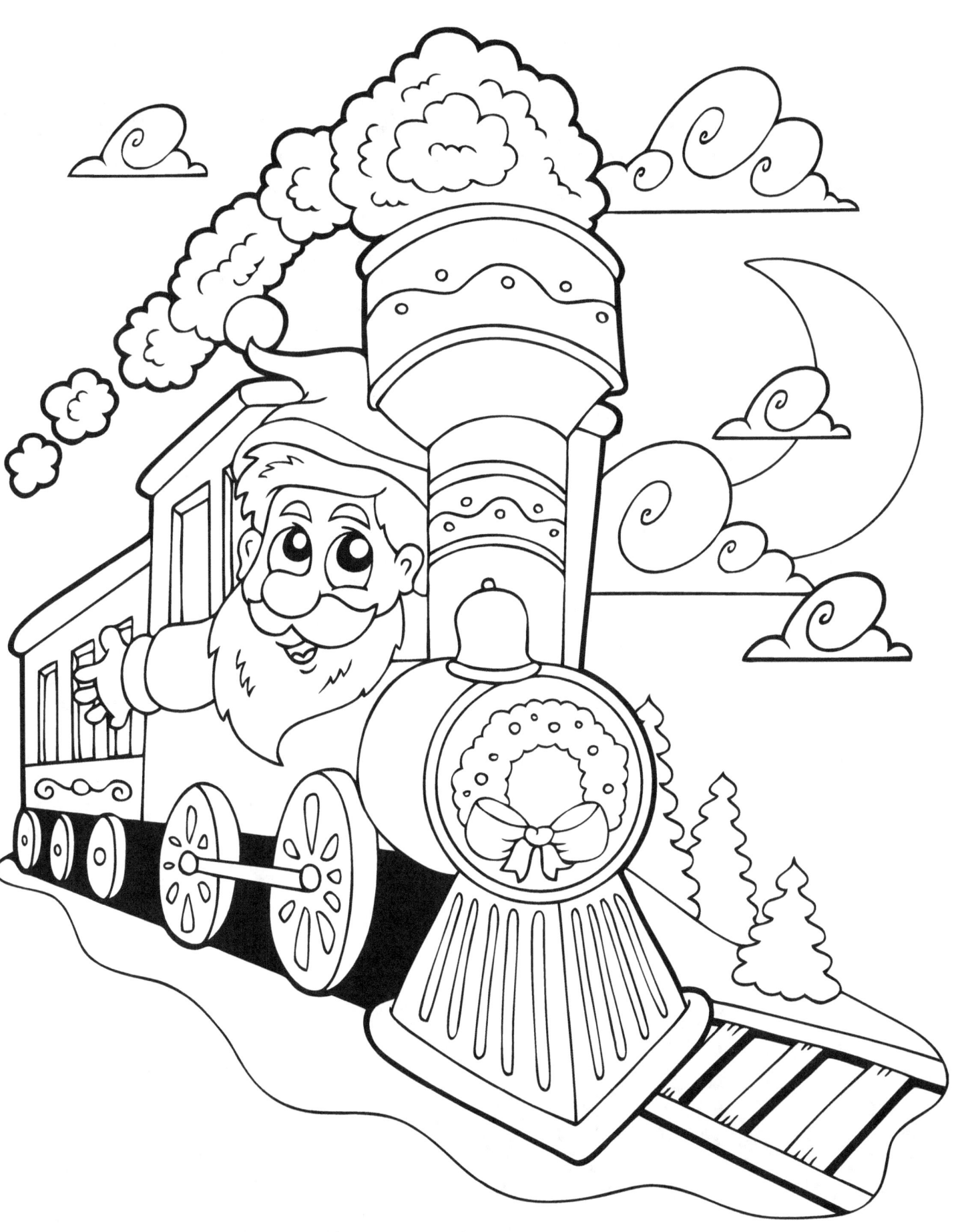

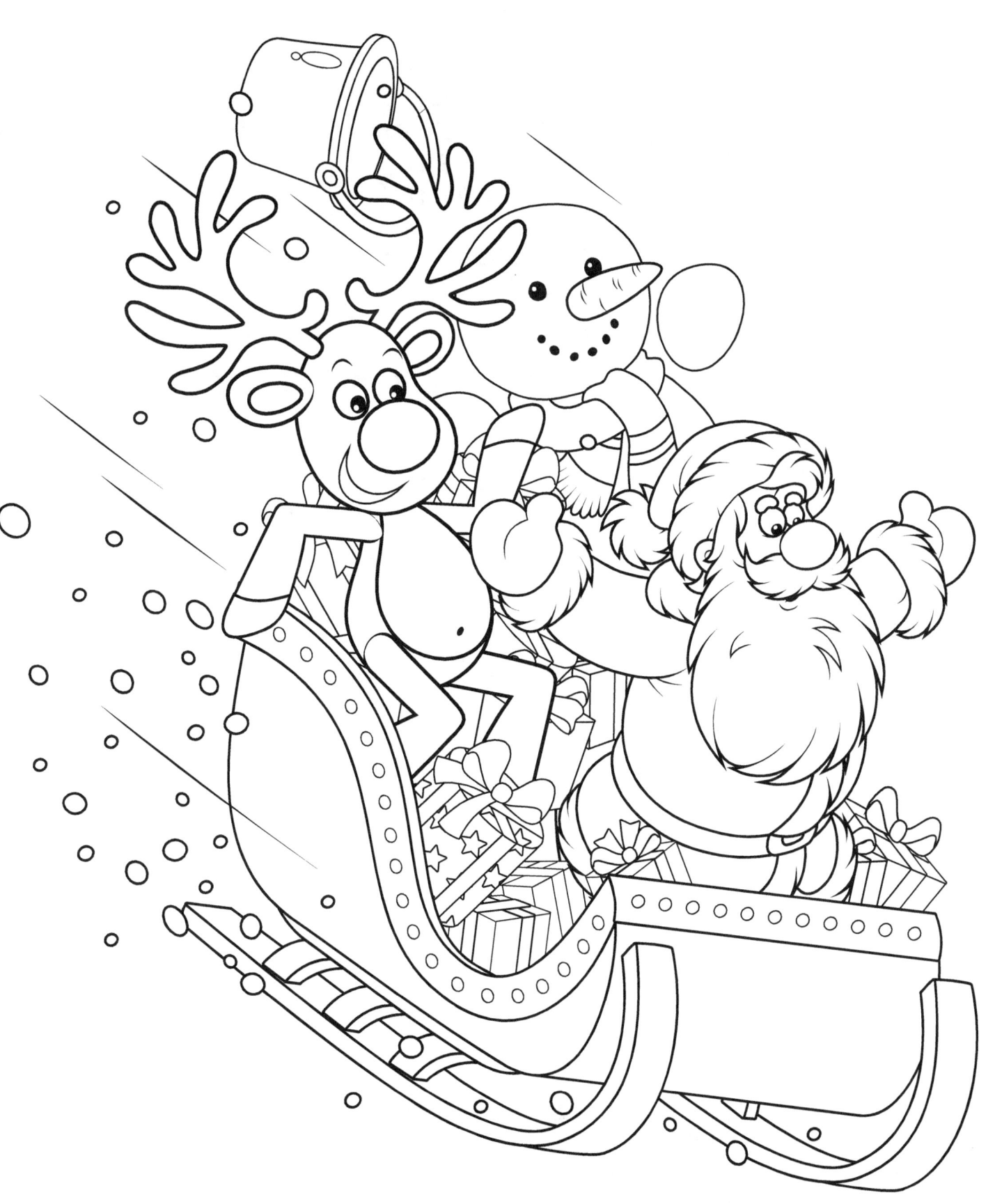

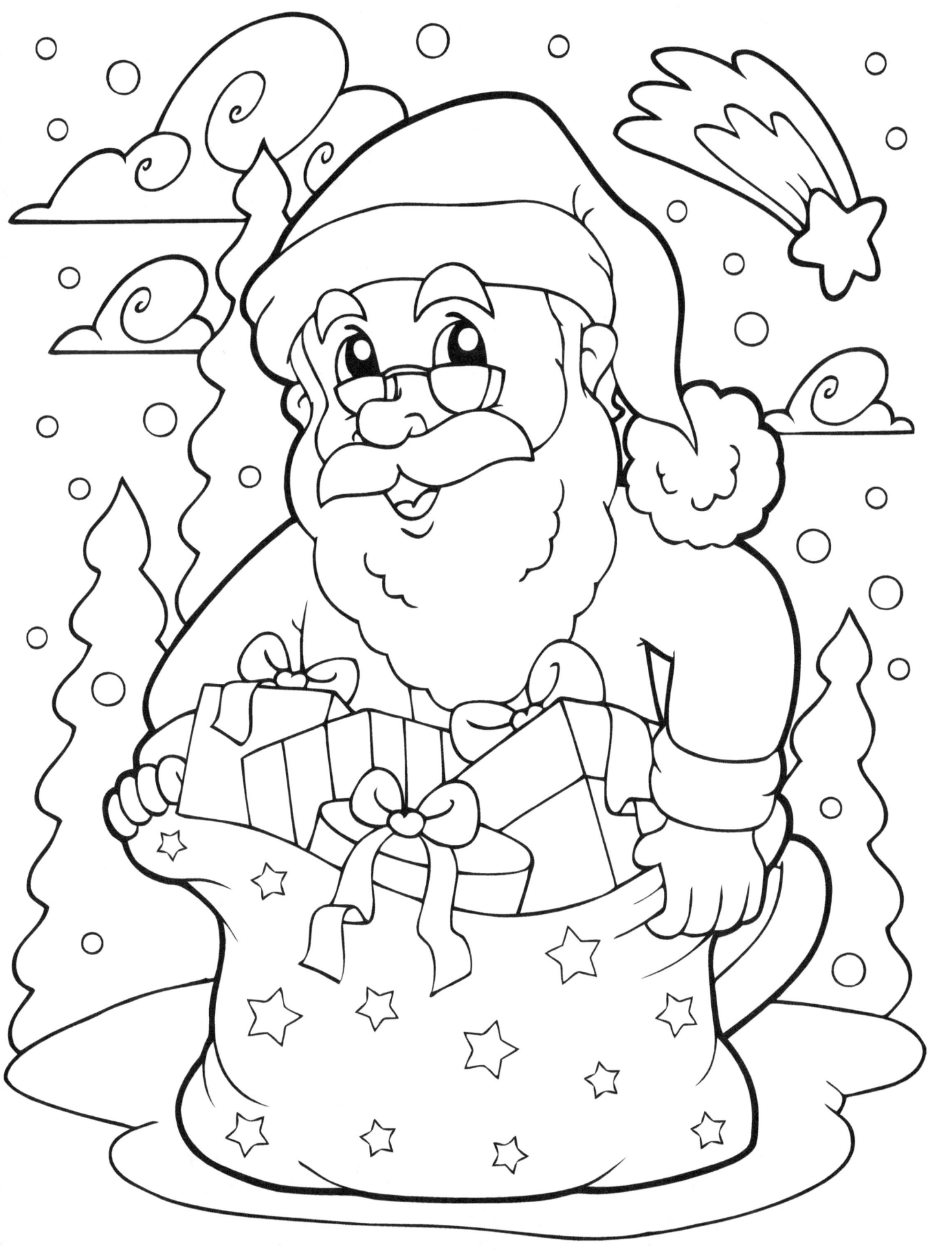

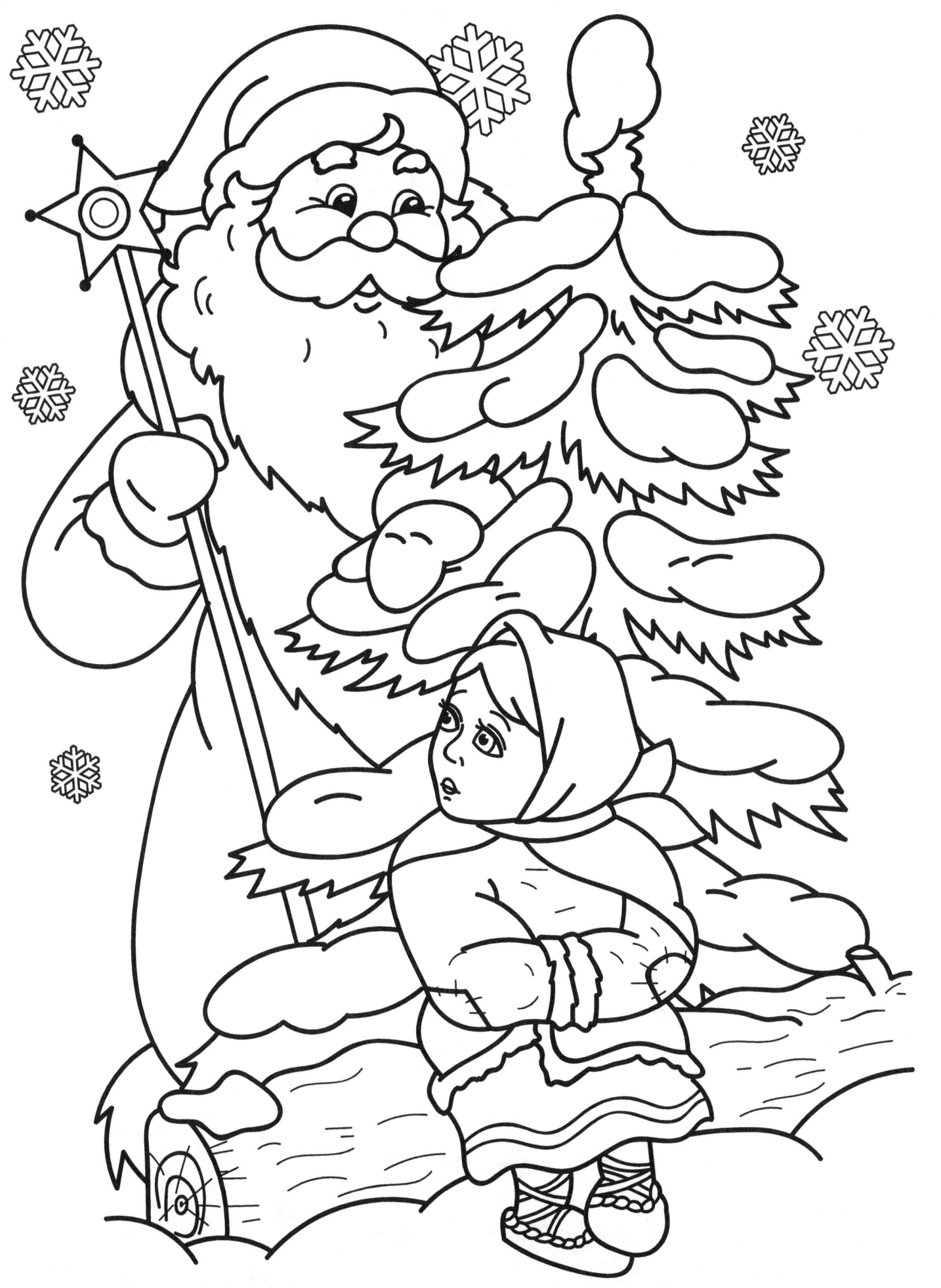

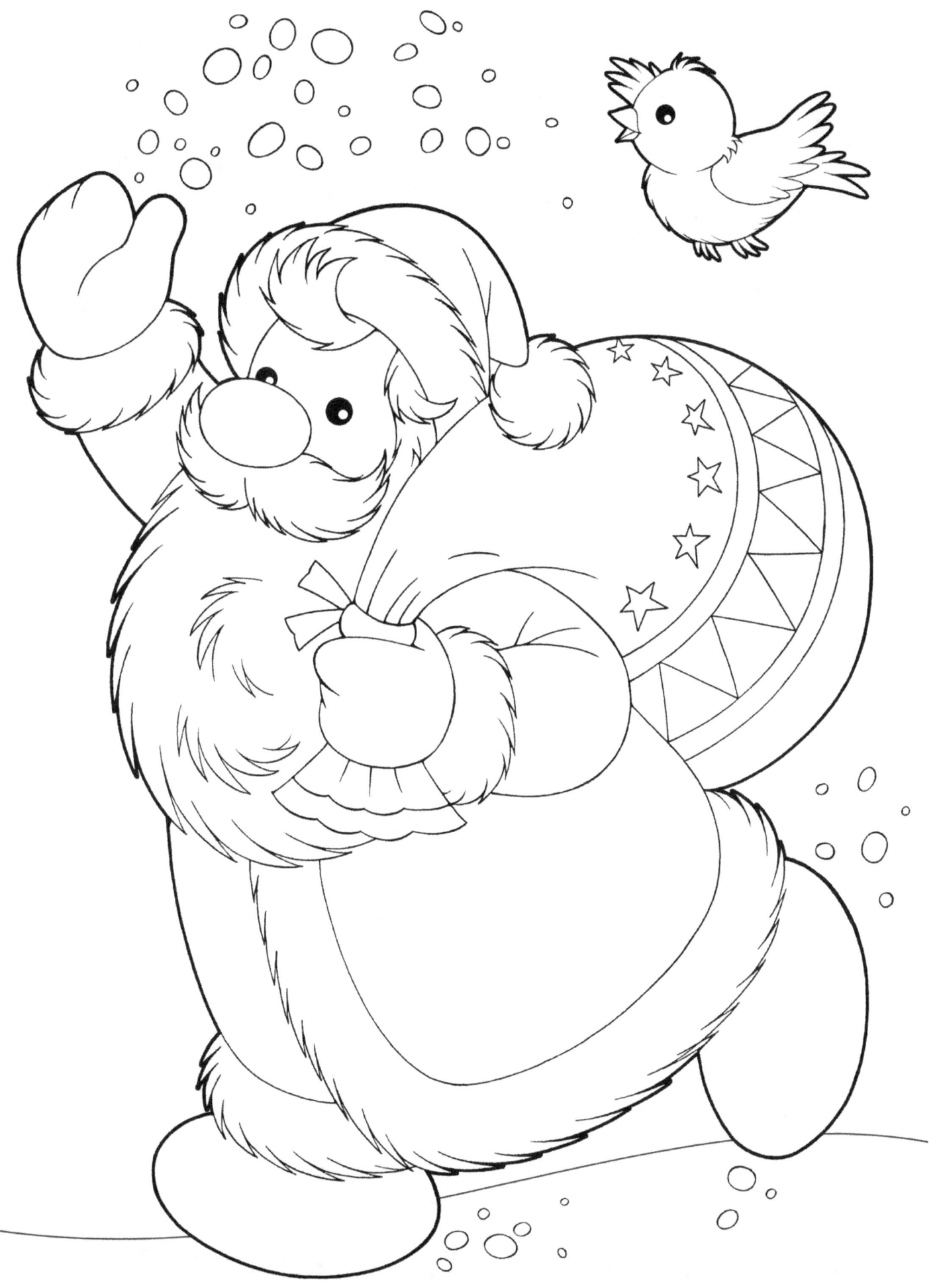

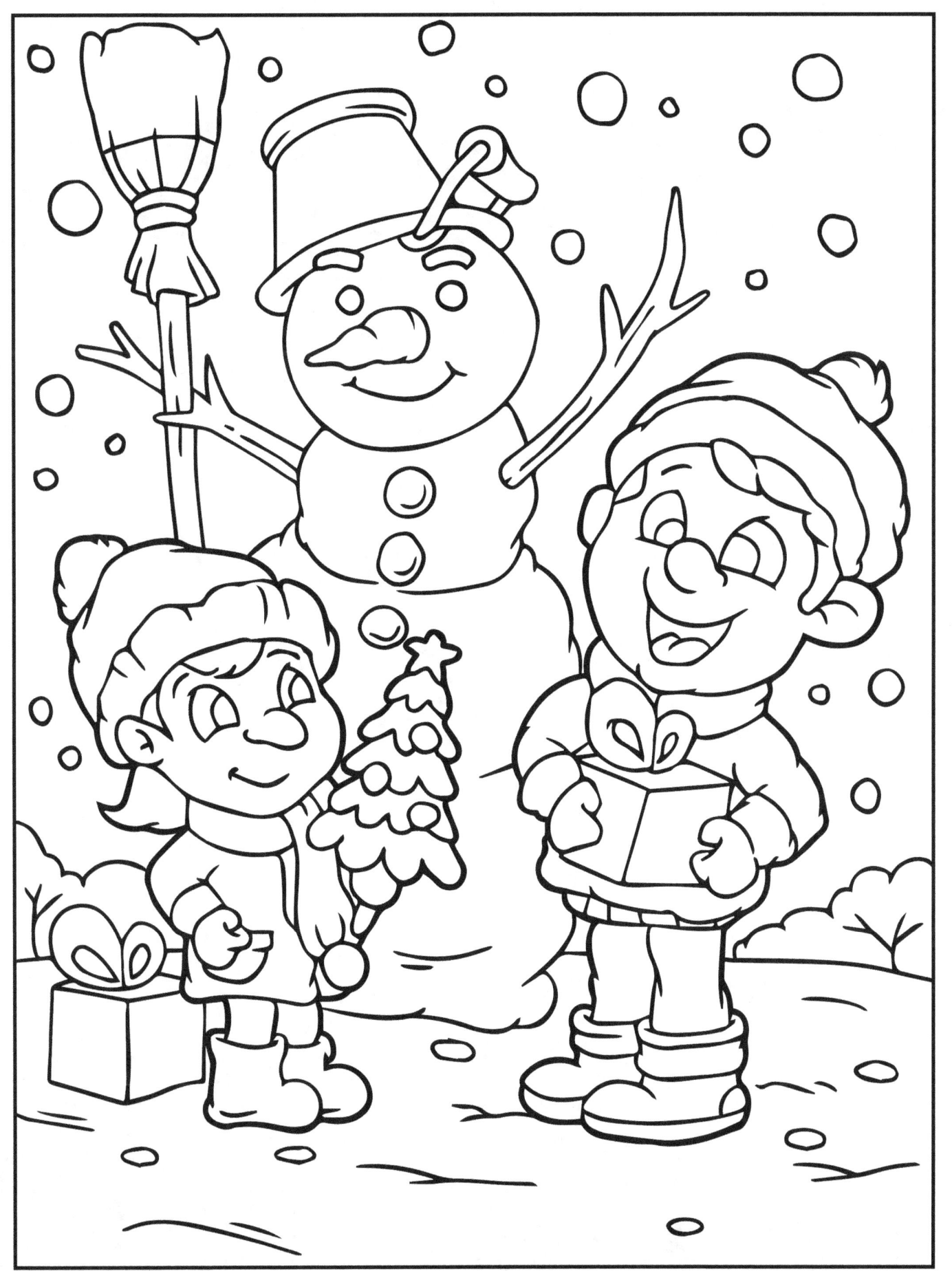

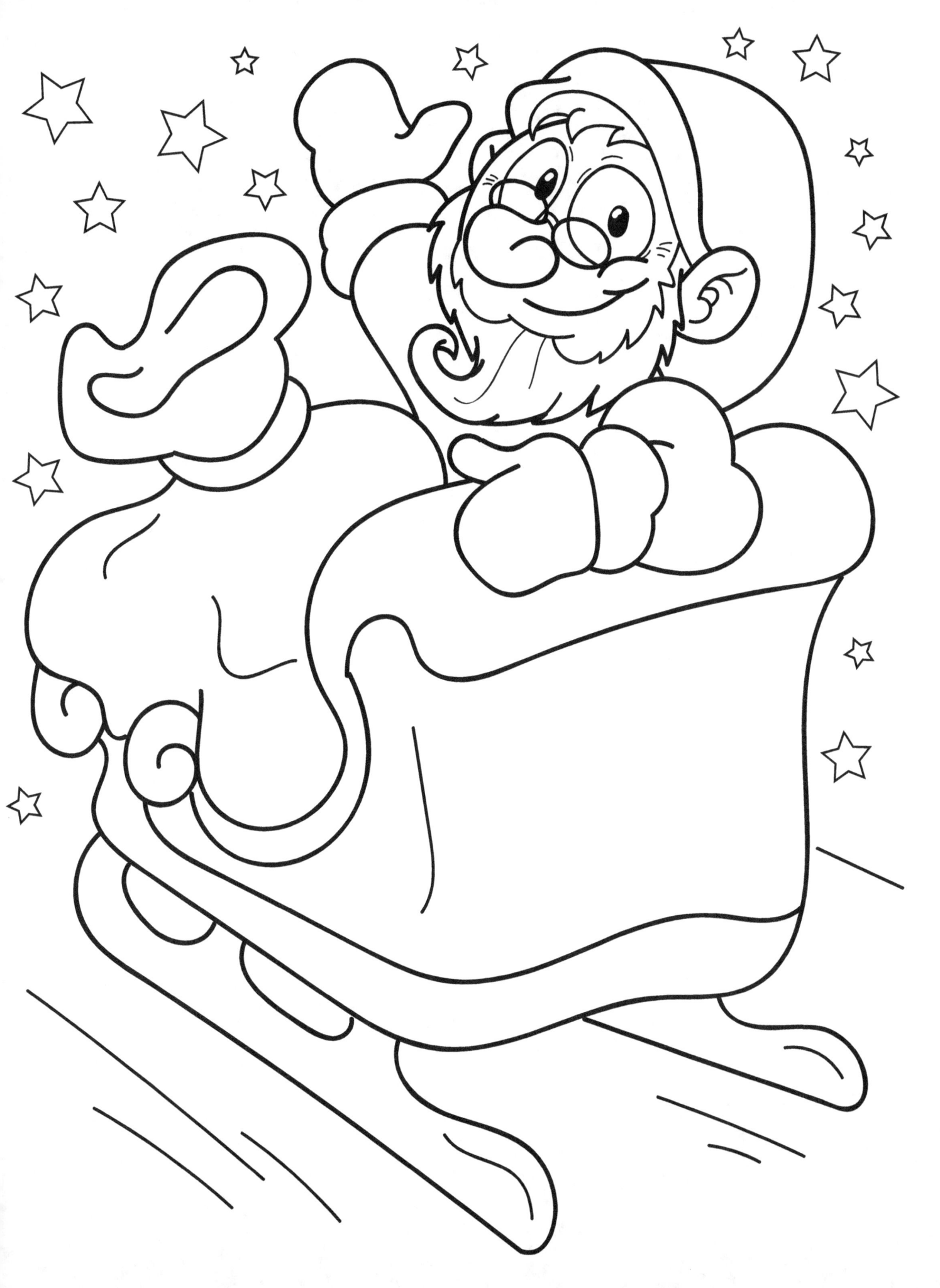

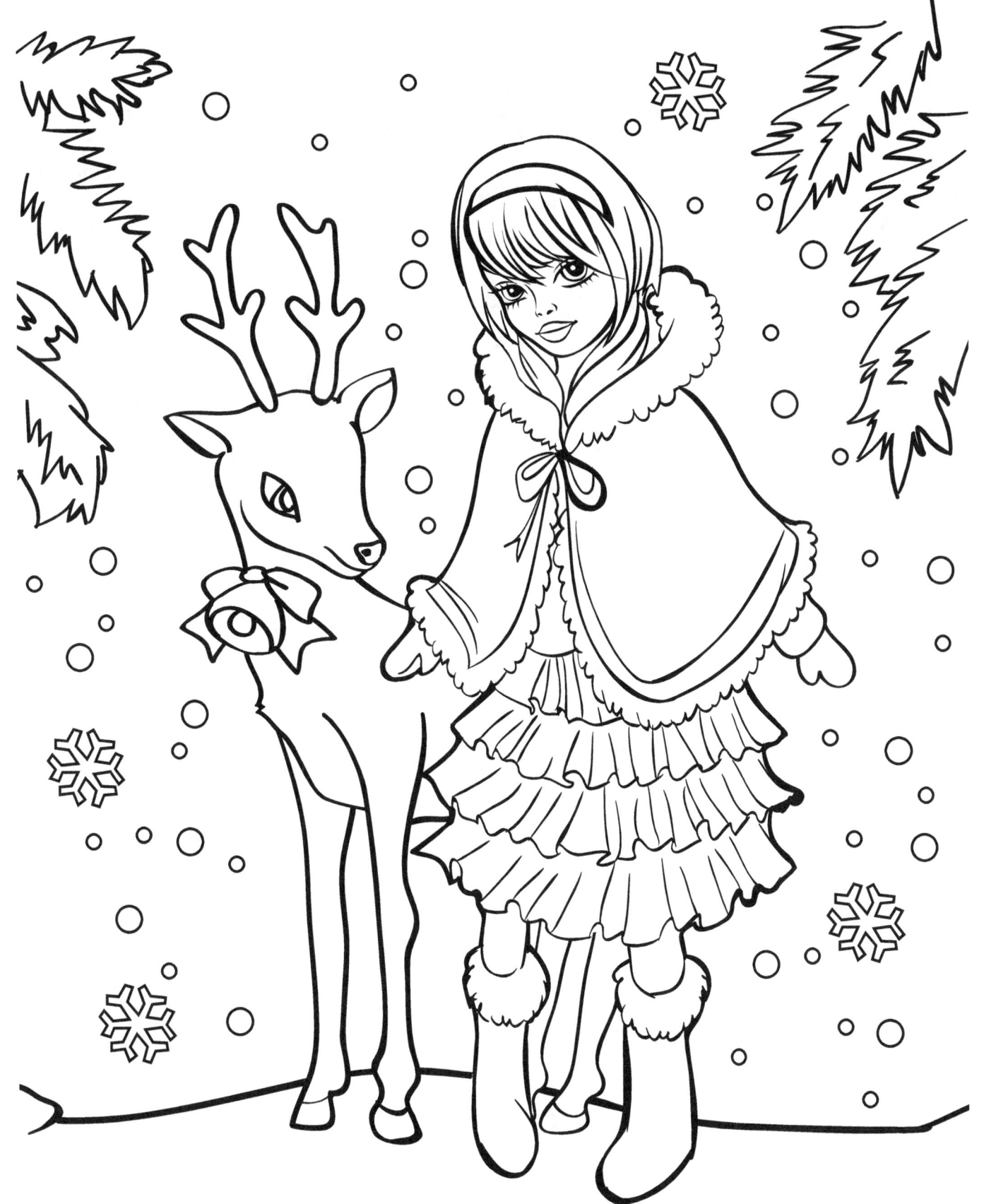

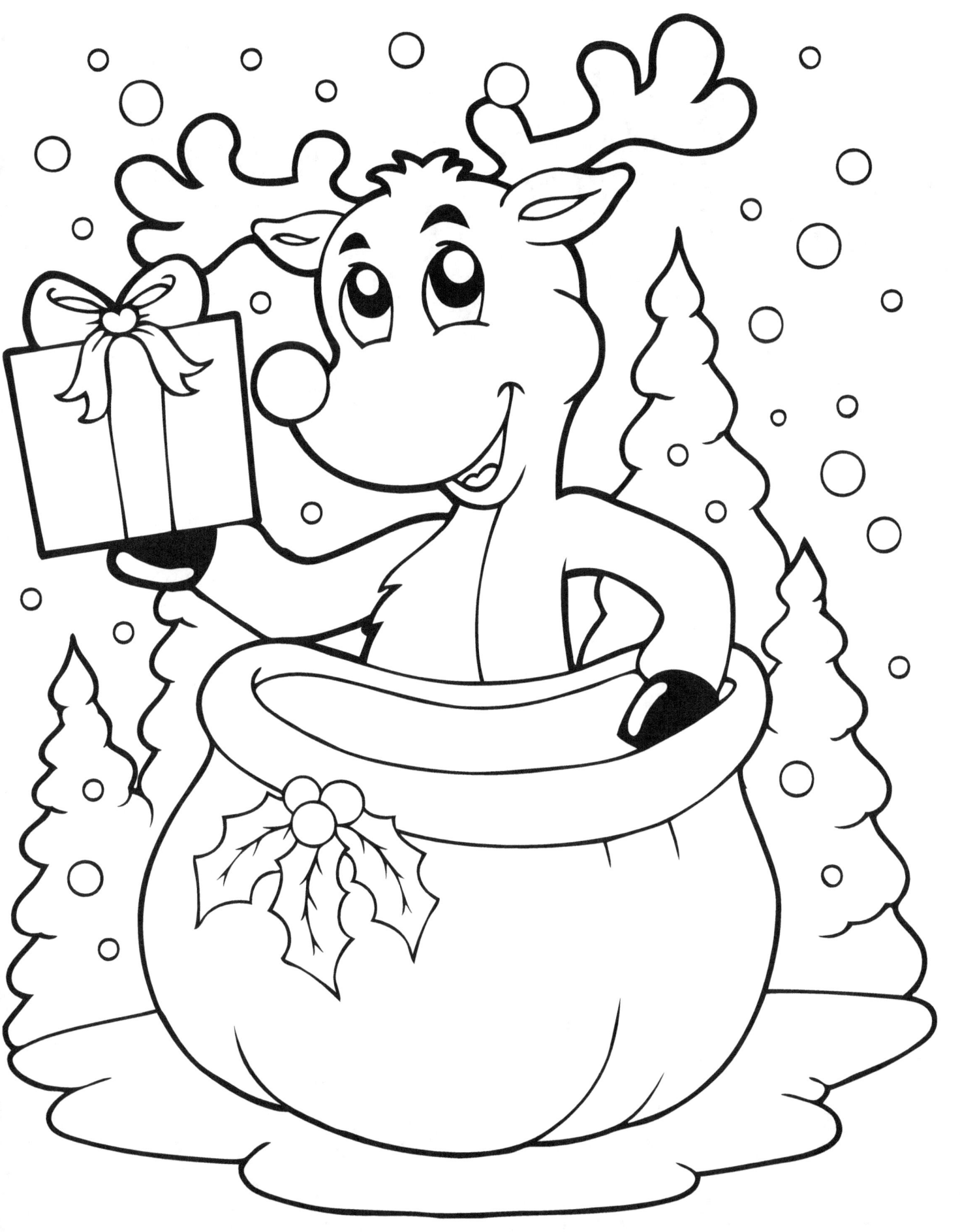

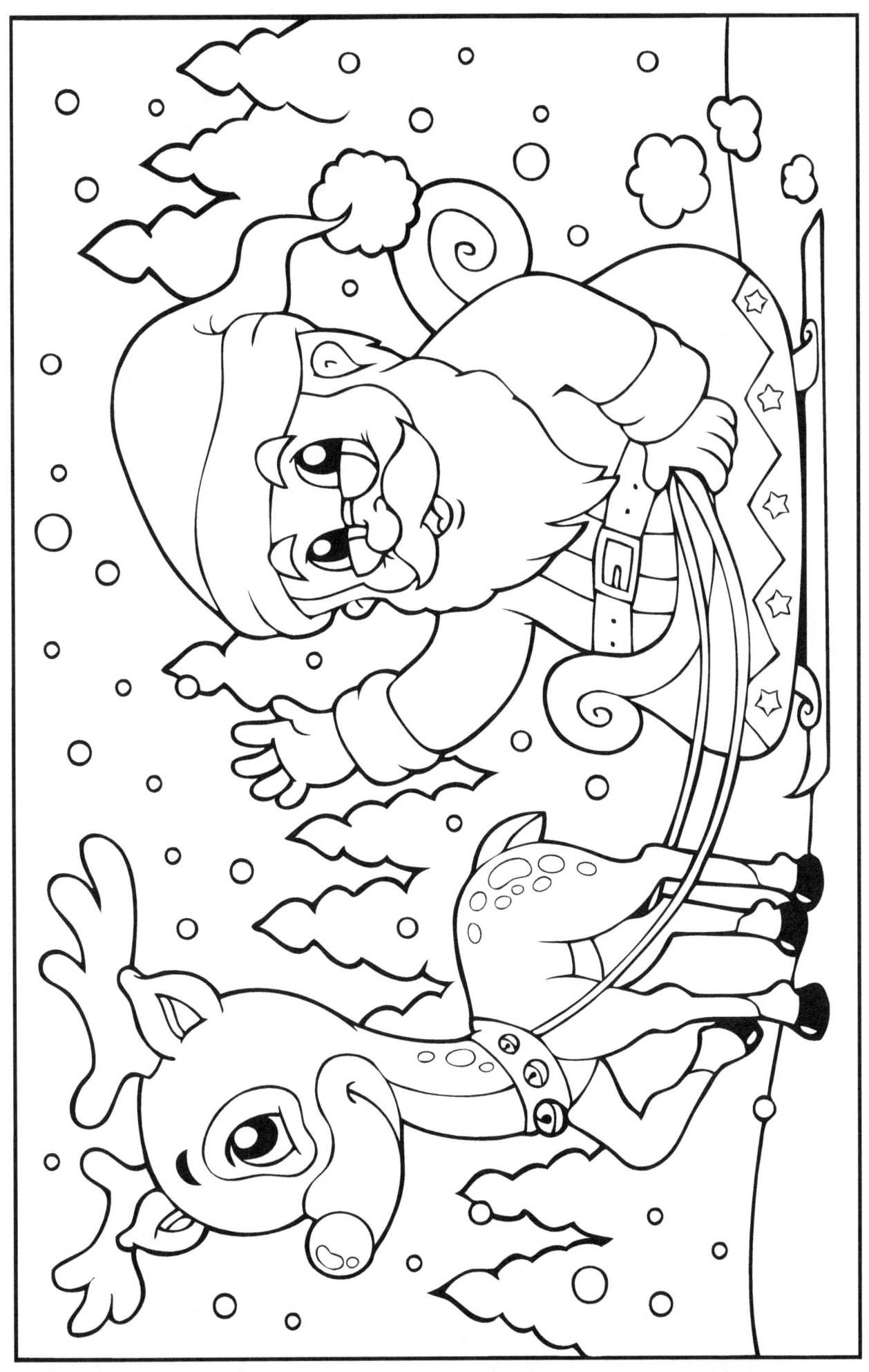

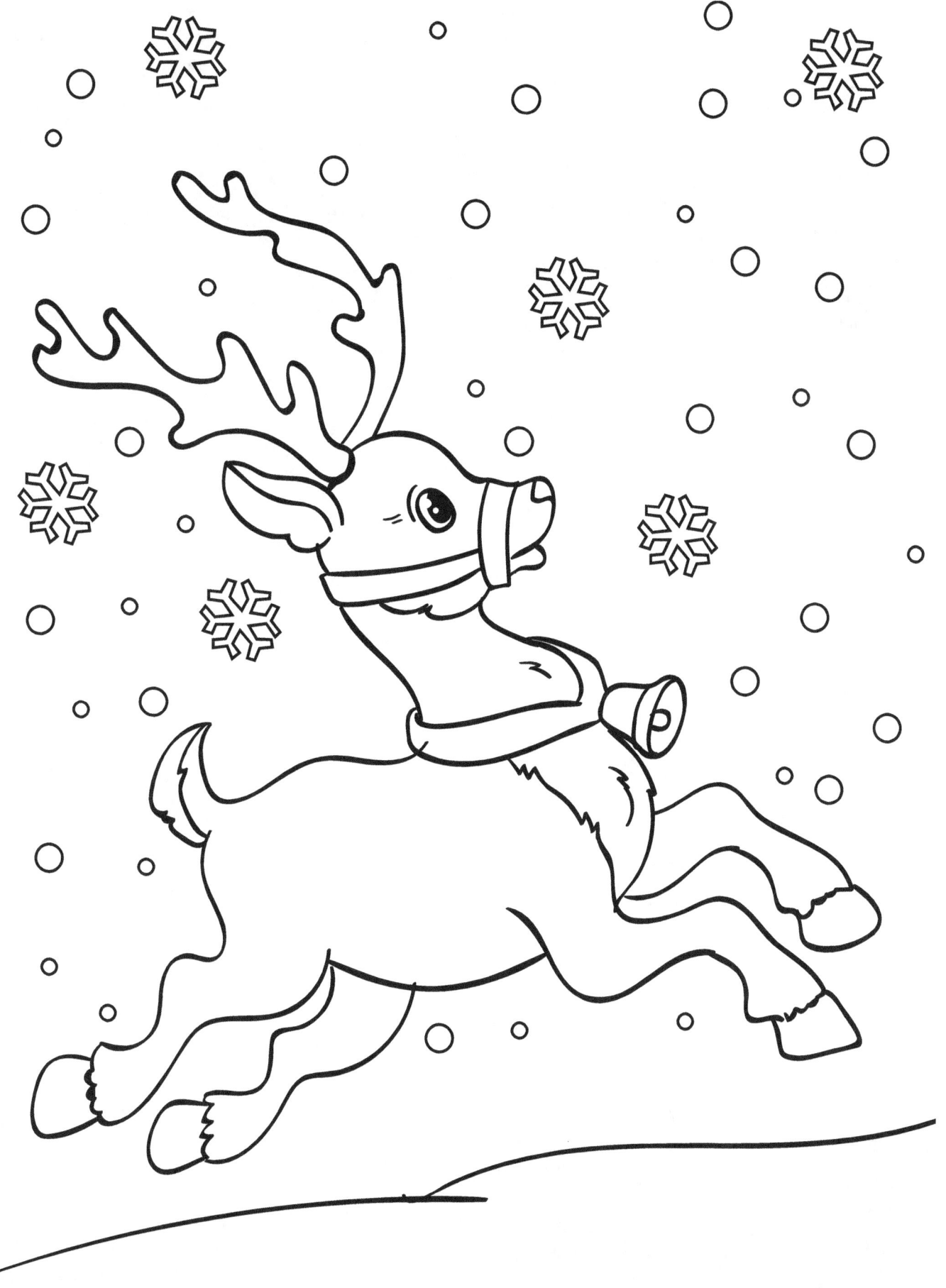

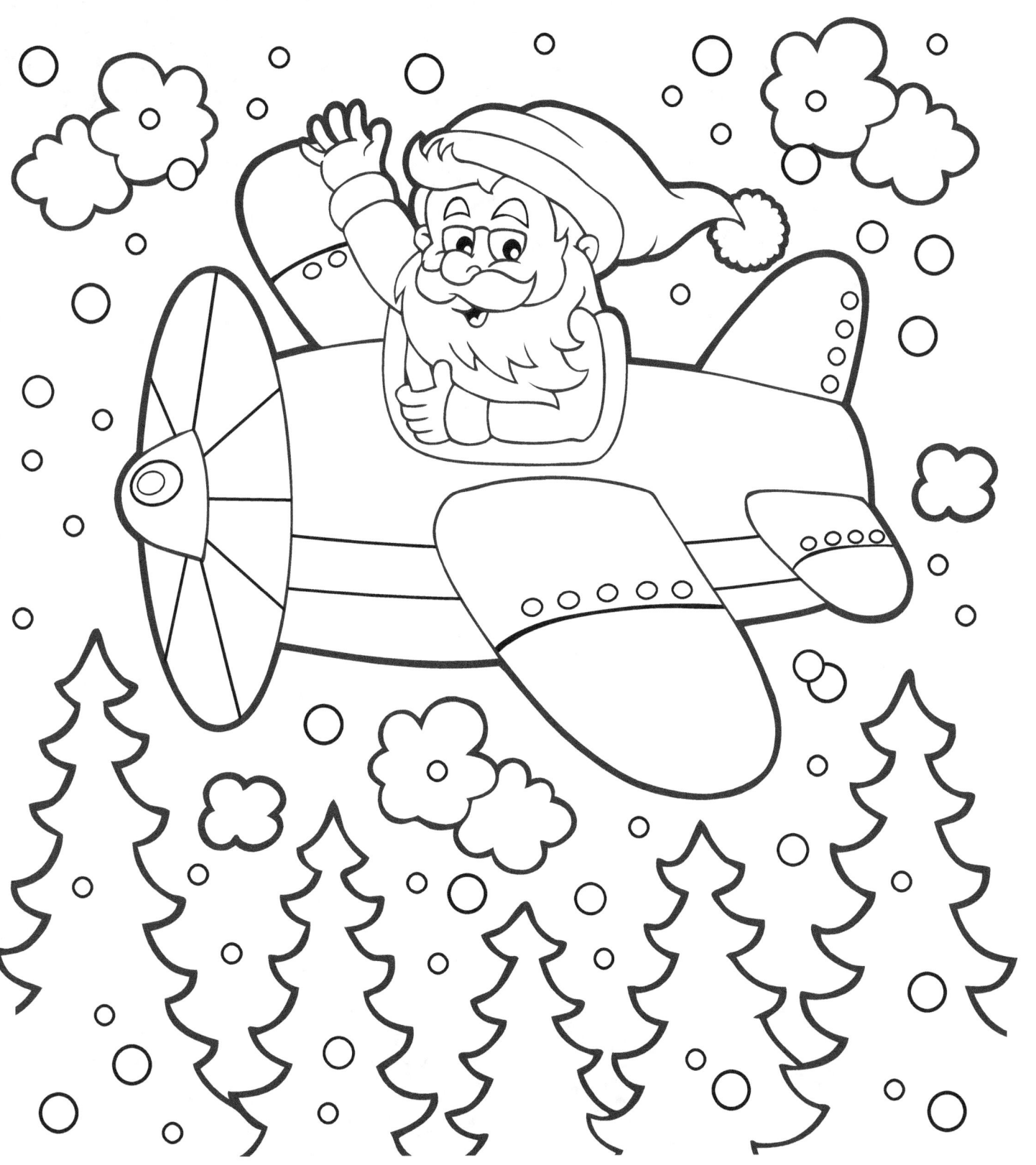

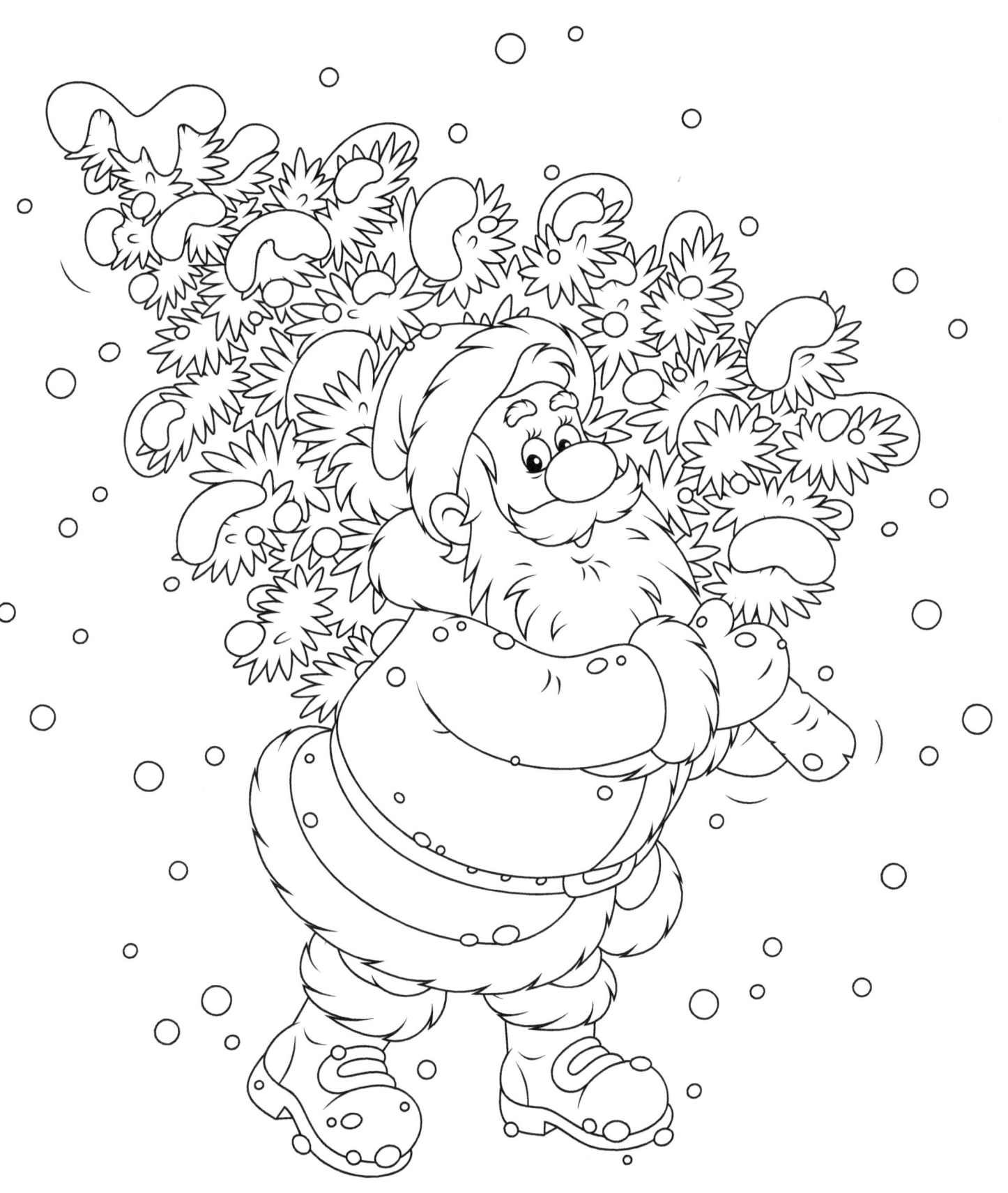

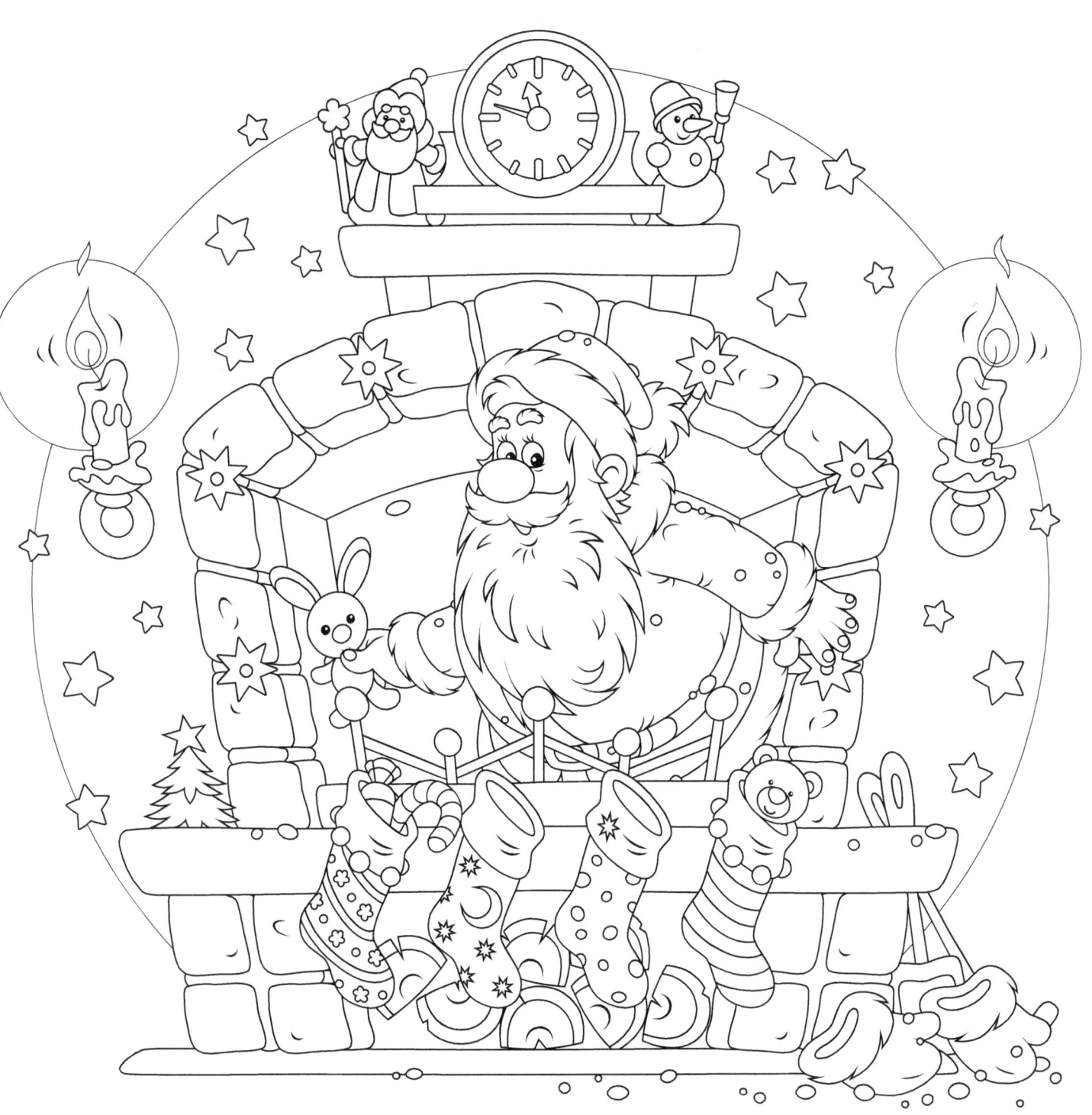

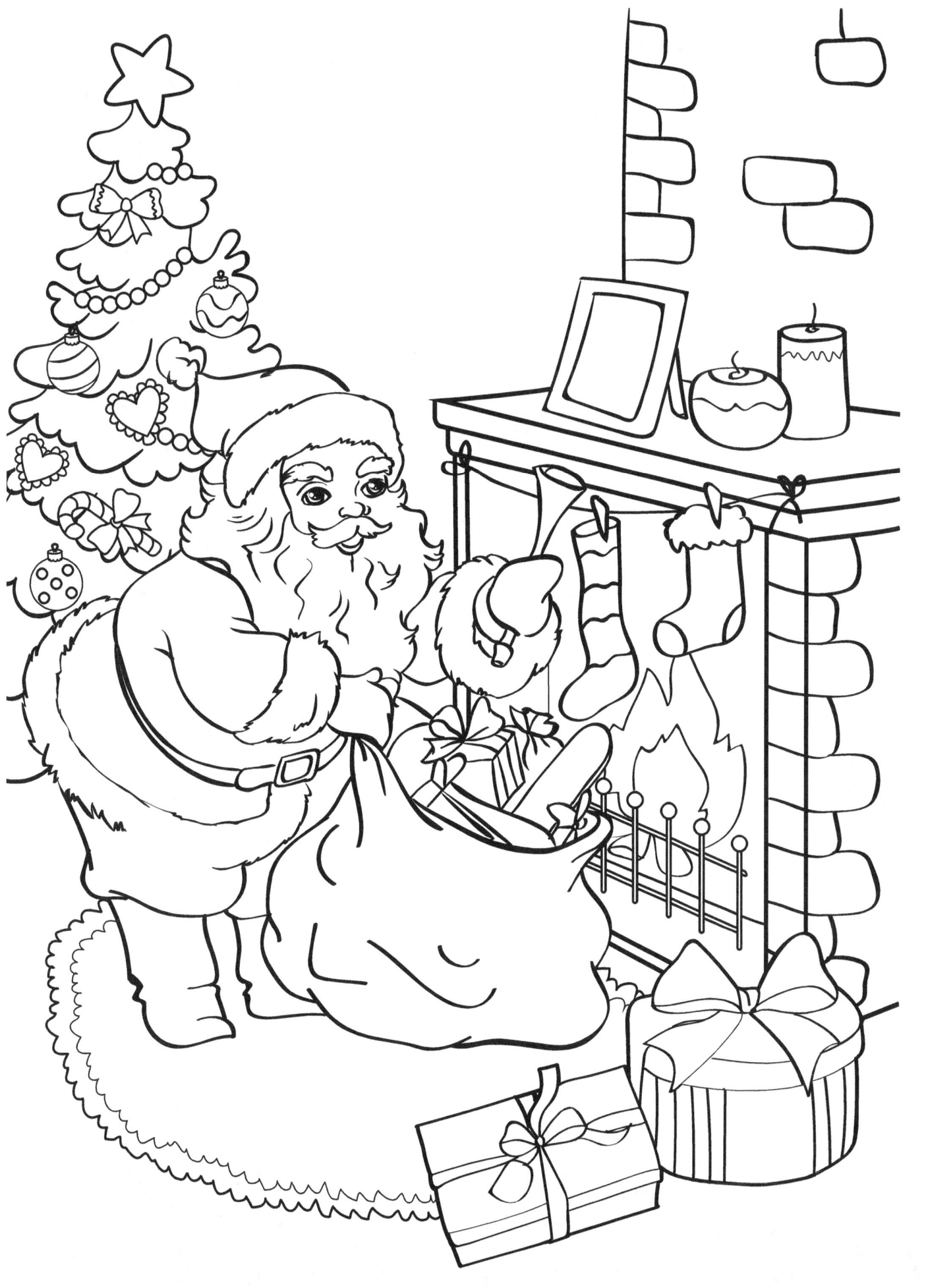

www.ingramcontent.com/pod-product-compliance
Lightning Source LLC
Chambersburg PA
CBHW080852220526
45467CB00008B/2480

* 9 7 8 1 7 0 6 6 3 2 8 8 7 *